Writers ARE Readers

FLIPPING READING INSTRUCTION INTO WRITING OPPORTUNITIES

Lester L. Laminack • Reba M. Wadsworth

HEINEMANN
Portsmouth, NH

Heinemann
361 Hanover Street
Portsmouth, NH 03801–3912
www.heinemann.com

Offices and agents throughout the world

Cataloging-in-Publication Data is on file at the Library of Congress.
ISBN: 978-0-325-05663-0

Editor: Holly Kim Price
Production: Victoria Merecki
Cover and interior designs: Suzanne Heiser
Front cover photos: Getty Images/Dorling Kindersley (top); Getty Images/Tetra Images/Daniel Grill (bottom)
Typesetter: Shawn Girsberger
Manufacturing: Steve Bernier

Printed in the United States of America on acid-free paper

19 18 17 16 15 VP 1 2 3 4 5

DEDICATION

For Norma Kimzey, a relentless and passionate advocate
for children and teachers, a dedicated educator,
a kind and gentle spirit, and a dear friend.

And in memory of Maryanne Manning, a mentor whose
influence lives on, a leader among teachers,
a gracious soul, and a dear friend.
You are cherished and missed.

CONTENTS

Acknowledgments vi

Introduction vii

Section 1: **Text Structure and Organization** 1

Chapter 1: Description 3

Chapter 2: Sequence 12

Chapter 3: Problem and Solution 21

Chapter 4: Compare and Contrast 29

Chapter 5: Cause and Effect 42

Section 2: **Weaving Meaning** 51

Chapter 6: Inferring 56

Chapter 7: Summarizing 68

Chapter 8: Synthesizing 78

Chapter 9: Visualizing 90

Chapter 10: Noticing Important Details 98

Chapter 11: Making Connections 107

Section 3: **Story Elements** 117

Chapter 12: Character 119

Chapter 13: Setting 128

Chapter 14: Plot 138

Chapter 15: Perspective and Point of View 146

Works Cited 157

ACKNOWLEDGMENTS

Writers ARE Readers: Flipping Reading Instruction into Writing Opportunities grew out of conversations with teachers who are devoted to making reading and writing instruction relevant and meaningful in a time of ever increasing standards and expectations. Your concern that instruction feels disjointed and leaves children thinking of reading and writing as unrelated activities actually launched this book. We are grateful to those teachers and literacy coaches who lingered after conference presentations, workshops, and professional development meetings to share their questions and stories. Your questions and concerns nudged us into our own conversations. We hope this book is evidence that we listened.

We are grateful to colleagues and friends who pushed our thinking, allowed us to work alongside them in their schools, offered insights and questions and conversations, helped us to gather writing samples, and helped to keep us focused on the young readers and writers working in classrooms every day. Thanks to Delicia Bell, Mary Alice Cagle, KK Cherney, Dana Cotney, Angie Diles, Mary Kay Hodges, Melanie Sutherland Holtsman, Nancy Johnson, Brenda Joyal, A.J. Maples, Matt Morris, Rachael Morris, Melissa Penley, Carrie Rohr, Suzanne Vermeire, Amanda McNeel Watson, and Felicia Woodruff.

A book is the result of the collective efforts of many beyond the authors. We are grateful to the team at Heinemann, who worked cheerfully and diligently to ensure that Writers ARE Readers: Flipping Reading Instruction into Writing Opportunities became a reality. We are grateful to our Heinemann editor, Holly Kim Price, for her guidance when we became too focused on a tree and lost sight of the forest. We are most grateful to those involved in the editorial, production, and marketing process. Thank you Lisa Fowler, Patty Adams, Victoria Merecki, Suzanne Heiser, and Sarah Fournier.

INTRODUCTION

Reading and writing are mutually supportive processes; therefore, gaining insight in reading deepens insight into writing and vice versa. For example, when a reader develops an understanding of a structure, an organizing principle, a reading strategy, or insights into the elements of story, she also gains a window into understanding how to assemble texts as a writer. This developing knowledge, especially if made explicit, will change the way she approaches texts as both reader and writer. Understanding reading gives the learner yet another way of making sense of the text unfolding in her mind as she reads. And it gives her a new set of options for creating texts as she writes.

When we teach addition and subtraction as inverse operations in mathematics, we lead the learner toward deeper conceptual understanding. We help her recognize that $4 + 3 = 7$ and therefore, $7 - 3 = 4$. When the learner comes to understand the reciprocal nature of subtraction and addition, each operation becomes clearer. Knowing how these two related operations are inextricably connected can only make for more efficient thinking in mathematics.

Similarly, in literacy, reading supports writing and writing supports reading, though we understand that as teachers our planning and instruction too often separate the two. As teachers, most of us can quickly put our hands on some reading program where lesson plans for reading are clearly described. Yet, writing is less frequently presented as a related activity. When reading and writing instruction are planned separately, each without regard for the other, the resulting instruction fails to weave clear connections between these related language processes. If our instruction separates reading from writing, then our students will be unlikely to think of the two as mutually supportive processes. The result is less efficient, perhaps less effective, reading-writing understandings, behaviors, and attitudes.

The most common exploration of the relationship between reading and writing tends to be a study of craft and the use of mentor texts. Craft study can be an effective way to enhance our students' control of written language, especially in terms of word choice, sentence structure, and organization or text structure. However, mentor texts are used too often only to highlight a craft technique, which is then assigned for student writers to employ. These titles will help you explore that work in greater depth and move beyond craft as an assignment:

- ◆ Ralph Fletcher and JoAnn Portalupi, *Craft Lessons: Teaching Writing K–8*
- ◆ Ralph Fletcher and JoAnn Portalupi, *Nonfiction Craft Lessons: Teaching Information Writing K–8*
- ◆ Lester L. Laminack, *Cracking Open the Author's Craft: Teaching the Art of Writing*
- ◆ Katie Wood Ray, *Wondrous Words: Writers and Writing in the Elementary School*

The focus of *Writers ARE Readers: Flipping Reading Instruction into Writing Opportunities* is to deepen our understanding of what we expect of readers, what we teach readers to do, how a reader's insights can be the pathway into a more thorough understanding of writing, and how we as teachers can flip those insights to lead students into a more robust understanding of what it means to be literate. We pursue the notion of helping students recognize reading and writing as mutually supportive processes to make their developing literacy more meaningful and efficient.

As teachers we recognize that each reader insight we help a learner grasp could be flipped and taught to a writer. It could be said that the writer must do something before the reader can take action. A writer constructed that "flip" (perhaps intuitively and without intention), and we can lead our students toward gaining those writer insights to inform their own work as writers. We have a long history of instruction designed to help the reader take action in the construction of meaning. Our focus here is to help readers see the flipside of those actions, gain insight into the writing behind them, and then activate those insights as writers.

Consider what may happen if we were to teach a reading strategy over time and watch it take hold in the life of a reader. As the reader begins to gain confidence and independence, we pose the notion that the writer had to do something to set that up on the page in some way. So we return to that text to explore the same segment with the lens of a writer, this time asking what the writer did to create the necessary situation for the reader. Leading the student to understand what he did as a reader then becomes a lens that brings into focus what the writer had to do before a reader ever saw the page. This insight (or flip) now becomes a teaching point in a writing lesson to be added to the student's repertoire.

Likewise we may begin with a writing lesson in which we focus our students' attention on the act of building a text. Perhaps we teach them to build tension in a scene or to foreshadow a big event with small, well-placed details. Whatever we make visible for our writers has a flipside for our readers as well. Consider learning about the concept of foreshadowing as a writer. As with any new insight, the student writer will likely play with his new understanding and use it widely, even poorly at first. But as he begins to focus his attention on appropriate use of this insight he will also very likely begin to focus attention on how it is used by others, especially if we guide his attention. Having learned the idea from the inside out gives him both *know how* and *know why*, which makes him an ever more savvy reader. Now when he begins to recognize the setup for foreshadowing an event, he also begins to expect and anticipate what is being foreshadowed. As it happens, these insights, when coupled, tend to escalate potential. For example, learning two ways to foreshadow as a writer may open his attention to the concept in general, so as a reader he begins to specifically notice those two ways to foreshadow. Before long he notices a third or fourth, and these new ways work their way into his writing repertoire. Soon he has acquired insight as a reader and control as a writer.

Another way to consider these connections is to think of the student's existing language and concepts, background knowledge, and schema as an investment account. (See Figure I.1.) Deposits are continuously made into that account as a student engages in reading and conversation, participates in experiences, and listens to music and stories and texts read aloud. Those deposits increase the holdings in the "account" through connections and associations as they link ideas together with existing concepts and language, creating more

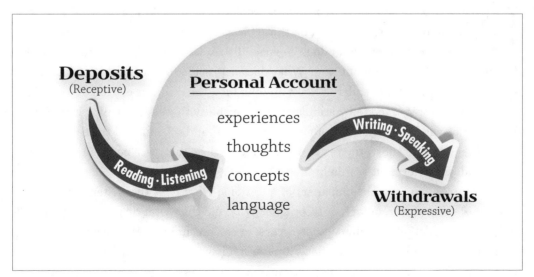

Figure I.1 Investing in Reader–Writers

thoughts and new possibilities. Reading, listening, engaging in experience, and thinking expand the known.

Speaking and writing draw upon what is on deposit; our vocabulary and our understanding of how to organize text or speech pull from that account. Unlike a bank account, it isn't diminished by use; rather it is increased. Yet, we teachers must be careful that our instructional expectations are not asking our students to "overdraw" on this account. That is to say, we can't expect our students to organize thoughts and articulate insights through talk or writing unless there are adequate holdings in the account in the form of conceptual development and vocabulary.

So we read aloud and host robust conversations about content and text structure and strategies and language. We set up opportunities for exploration and experience to build or strengthen conceptual development and vocabulary. We present information and texts and experiences that offer multiple points of view through various text types and media. And we lift and make visible the mutually supportive roles of reading and writing. When we teach reading we reveal the flipside in writing.

Making a Flip

The basic notion is simple. As we wrote this book we began making a list of what we typically teach to readers. Then we took those ideas and strategies one by one and asked: What does this require? What does it expect the reader to know, do, or possess? What does it assume the reader will bring? What does it provide for the reader? For example, when the text expects the reader to make an inference, the reader is expected to possess a schema for the topic, a related vocabulary, and the ability to weave meaning between the threads he brings from his own thoughts, experiences, and schema and the threads given him by the writer. In short, the reader is expected to close the space between what is presented and what is present within him.

To set up the flip we ask a similar set of questions: What does the writer have to know in terms of content, vocabulary, or technique? What did the writer do to set up the conditions for the reader? What language, structure, or craft technique was involved?

In our example with inference, the writer doesn't have to make an inference; rather she has to imply or allude. She has to set up the reader to make an inference. The writer has several options here. She can offer suggestions or hints without revealing the telling detail.

She may allude to cultural knowledge or another text, choose a metaphor or simile, or use figurative language to leave the reader with adequate threads. The reader must weave those in with his own knowledge and vocabulary as he begins weaving meaning and closing the space between what has been presented by the writer and what is present within. Like the reader, the writer must also have a schema for the topic and a command of the language needed to convey her intentions. In addition, she must have an awareness of the audience and what those readers may (or may not) know.

The idea of a flip is simple: Heads you read, tails you write. On one side we think about what is expected of the reader. We focus on what he must do to make meaning for himself. On the other side we think about what the writer had to do to set up the reader. We often ask readers, "So let's return to that spot and think about what the writer did that helped you make sense of that." Our focus on the writer in these situations does not diminish the importance of what the reader brings to the text. In our view, this attention deepens the process of making meaning by helping the reader gain insight into how the process works. And, of course, there is the added benefit of equipping the student writer with an opportunity to peer through the process and see into the other side.

Try it for yourself. Think about a typical reading strategy. Let's think about visualizing. Begin by thinking about what visualizing expects of the reader. Make a list of those expectations. Now flip it and think about what the writer had to do to set up the situation for the reader. List those. Now think about lifting ideas and making instruction from them.

Visualizing expects the reader to:

The writer set this up by:

So let's dig in a bit and explore what we teach our readers and consider how we could take each teaching point and "flip it" for writing instruction.

Schema

Schema is a word that buzzes around in conversations about comprehension. Dictionaries say that a schema is a plan, a structured framework, or way of organizing. All that information in our minds isn't just floating around randomly; even if we aren't aware of it, that information is organized.

We humans do like getting organized. Just think about our closets. Closets are places where we store what we plan to use later. Most of us have some scheme for organizing our closets so we can find what we need. There are lots of ways to organize a closet. Some people choose to organize everything by color. Others organize by season, winter clothes packed away and spring/summerwear hanging and ready for use. Some may prefer to organize by function, having a section for leisure, one for formal wear, a space for work clothes, and another for working in the yard.

If you know him well, you'd not be surprised to know that Lester's closet is organized by color, moving from the darkest shade to the lightest. So what happens when he goes shopping and comes home with a new shirt that isn't just one color? What if he comes home with plaids or stripes or paisleys or some other print? Lester lays the shirt across the bed, steps back to see which color emerges as dominant, and places it in the just right spot among other shirts in that color section. The new shirt is *assimilated* into the existing scheme for organizing his closet.

However, if Lester were to bring home a shirt with a color or pattern that simply didn't fit into any of the existing categories in his closet, he'd have to make a new section for that shirt. In other words, he'd have to *accommodate* the existing scheme to add a section with new criteria.

It's fair to say that Lester has a schema for closets. That is, he has a system for organizing the coming and going of garments across time. That schema provides order and a sense of balance for him. It allows him to add new items when purchases are made. It allows for the storage and retrieval of garments easily as he packs or unpacks for travel when working with schools around the country. And if moving into a new home, his schema would enable him to set up the closets with ease.

A schema, then, is a system for organizing that makes storage and retrieval more efficient. Think for a moment about things we keep organized: a file cabinet, bookshelves, kitchen cabinets, or a silverware drawer. We have schema for each of these. When a young child is helping to do the dishes and opens the silverware drawer, there may be a tray with divided compartments for each item, making it easy for the child to place the spoons, forks, and knives back into their respective spots. However, when handed a serving spoon the child may pause, just like Lester bringing home a shirt that stretches his existing organizing plan for his closet. The child is likely to either add the larger serving spoon in with the smaller ones or ask, "Where does this big spoon go?"

Our schema helps us create order, make meaning, set up categories, link connections, and recognize patterns. As reader-writers we have a schema for how written language works, we have a schema for text types and text structures, and we have a schema for language patterns. As readers and writers, that schema helps us anticipate, predict, infer, and imply. It helps us construct, create, and generate new texts. It is an essential aspect of becoming and being a literate person. A schema helps us sort and find the information we need to make meaning, whether we are engaging with existing texts or generating new ones.

A schema is essential to readers because it enables them to find a home for new information, to fit it into the fabric evolving as they interact with texts. It gives the reader a sense of the pattern, a sense of order that guides his approach to the text as well as his engagement with the text.

Writers need a schema as well. A schema serves as the blueprint for the text being created. It enables the writer to imagine what the evolving text will look like when completed; it provides a point of reference for constructing the text. A schema provides the writer with a sense of structure and appropriate word choice to communicate more clearly. It gives the writer a "blueprint" of sorts for the genre she has chosen, the style appropriate to her purposes, and the voice that may best serve her intentions.

Moving Through the Book

It is our hope that this book makes the connections between reading and writing both visible and accessible. We share our thinking about flipping reading insights into writing opportunities in each section so that you will have a model that will enable you to examine your reading instruction and find other opportunities to flip for your students.

This book is organized into three broad sections:

- ◆ Text Structure
- ◆ Weaving Meaning
- ◆ Story Elements

In each section we examine ideas first through the lens of reading. We explore what the reader does, then think about how the writer helped set up the conditions necessary for that to happen. We offer a sample lesson for tapping into the reader insights then take that information and flip it to examine how a student could bring that new insight into his writing. A writing lesson is also provided as an example of our thinking. We share writing samples from classrooms and teachers from kindergarten through fifth grade who have tried this work. We know that you may not have the exact book we use in each lesson, so we end each chapter with a list of additional texts.

In the first section, Text Structure and Organization, we look into five basic text structures.

- ◆ Description
- ◆ Sequence
- ◆ Problem and Solution
- ◆ Compare and Contrast
- ◆ Cause and Effect

The second section, Weaving Meaning, is a close look at six commonly taught comprehension strategies.

- ◆ Inferring
- ◆ Summarizing
- ◆ Synthesizing
- ◆ Visualizing
- ◆ Determining Importance
- ◆ Making Connections

And in the final section, Story Elements, we focus on the common elements of story.

- ◆ Character
- ◆ Setting
- ◆ Plot (with attention to conflict and tension)
- ◆ Perspective and Point of View

TEXT STRUCTURE AND ORGANIZATION

When we talk about text structure we are talking about the ways writers organize their thoughts, both within and across a text. It may be the overarching framework for a textbook, an essay, a how-to book, or a story. It may also be the framework for a particular scene in a novel or for a specific segment of a chapter in an information book. While there is usually some framework for the text as a whole, it is not uncommon for a single text to employ more than one text structure.

Writing needs organization. Organization helps a reader make meaning from what is written. When the reader is aware of the text structure being used, it helps him organize his thoughts as he proceeds through the text. Text structure, then, gives the reader a way of understanding how information holds together and how ideas relate to one another.

Texts may be organized in several ways. Some of the more common text structures include:

- ◆ Description—details and examples, sensory information (e.g., *All the Places to Love* by Patricia MacLachlan)

- ◆ Sequence—steps in a process, events in a story, information, timeline/chronology (e.g., *Cookie's Week* by Cindy Ward)

- ◆ Problem Solution—the problem is presented and the solution unfolds across the text (e.g., *Enemy Pie* by Derek Munson)

- Compare and Contrast—showing how things are alike, showing how things are different (e.g., *Who Would Win? Killer Whale vs. Great White Shark* by Jerry Pallotta)
- Cause and Effect—what happened and why it happened (e.g., *If You Give a Mouse a Cookie* by Laura Joffe Numeroff)

1

DESCRIPTION

Description describes; it pulls us closer for a better look, it lets us listen in on conversations and music and laughter and the sound of things. Description guides our hands to know the feel of things, the hot and cold of them, the soft and smooth, the rough and prickly feel. Description makes your mouth pucker when it is focused on a lemon and makes your heart race when it is in a desperate situation. Description can make you sit up and take notice, slow down and lean in to attend to the very small, to see what you may often fail to recognize. Description takes us along on the journey. Description helps us know more about the subject; it fills us in with details and offers examples and gives us explanations. In descriptive writing a writer may move from the general to the specific, first naming the general category (honeybees) followed by specific attributes (like all insects, the honeybee has three body parts and six legs). Then as the text unfolds the writer will use descriptive writing to reveal the attributes of the honeybee. Description can move the reader forward through the text.

◄ LESSON FOCUS Introduce Description as a Text Structure

Readers, we are exploring different ways writers organize texts to help us make sense of what we read. Today we are going to explore description as a way to organize writing. When writers use description to organize their work for readers, they may tell us the subject and follow that with examples that describe the subject.

Let's return to a few of the books we have read about honeybees. You will remember this Weekly Reader book, *Bees*. Let's take a look at this page. [Turn to page 12.] The writer says, "Each bee has a job to do." So we know the writer is going to tell us about jobs the bees have. As we read on we find out, "Drones mate with the queen. The queen spends her life laying eggs. Worker bees raise the young. They gather food and guard the colony."

Notice how the writer told us the subject (bee jobs) and then tells us what those jobs are (1. drones mate with the queen, 2. the queen lays eggs, 3. workers raise the young, gather food, and guard the colony). Let's make a note of that.

The subject:

⬍ Jobs for bees

Description:

⬍ Drones mate with the queen.

⬍ The queen lays eggs.

⬍ Workers raise the young, gather food, and guard the colony.

I'm going to turn the page and read the first sentence. Listen and decide what the writer is going to describe next. "The bees live in a *hive*." What subject is the writer going to describe in the next few sentences? [Pause for their responses.]

Yes, the writer is going to describe what a hive is. I'll make a note of that for us.

Let's read on. "Inside the hive, worker bees build tiny wax rooms. The rooms are called *cells*. The honeybees store food in some cells. In other cells, they raise young bees."

Let's pause here and think about what we learned from the writer's description. Remember on this page the writer is telling us about a hive. [Pause to allow students to think and talk with a partner.] Readers, let me hear from a few of you. I'll jot down what we learned about a hive from the descriptions.

The subject:

⬍ The hive

Description:

⬍ Where bees live.

⬍ Tiny wax rooms called cells.

⬍ Honeybees store food in the cells.

⬍ Honeybees raise their young in the cells.

Readers, continue to think about how writers use description to help us understand and make sense when we are reading. We will visit this again.

▶ LESSON FOCUS Exploring Description as Readers

R eaders, we have been digging into structure and looking for the ways writers organize their texts to help us make sense of what we read. Recently we revisited *Bees* and noticed how the writer used descriptive writing to introduce the subject and tell us more.

Today I have another book you will remember from our bee study. This one is *The Honey Makers* by Gail Gibbons. We decided this is an information book that tells us all about one kind of bee, the honeybee. Gail Gibbons gives us drawings and captions and labels to help us understand, but she also uses descriptive writing.

Remember when we explored *Bees* we decided that in descriptive writing the writer will tell us the big idea, or the subject, and then give us more information to help us understand. That extra information may be examples or an explanation that describes the subject.

Let's turn to this page where the bees are working in the hive. [Turn to the page where brood cells are described.] As I read this page aloud I'd like you to listen for the big idea, or subject, on this page and notice how Gail Gibbons tells us more with descriptive writing.

> *Most cells in the beehive are used for storing honey, but some are used for the queen to lay her eggs. There are called brood cells. In each brood cell, a bee will develop and grow. The largest brood cells are queen brood cells, also called royal cells. Drone brood cells are smaller. Even smaller are the worker brood cells.*

Readers, think about what we just read. Pause and think about the subject and the description that tells us more. [Pause briefly while they sit and think.] Now turn to your partner, and share your thoughts about this page. [Again, pause briefly. Typically 40 to 50 seconds is enough.]

Readers, let me hear from a few of you. What did you decide is her big idea, or subject, for this section? [Pause for comments and make notes.]

The subject:

- ◆ Cells in the hive
- ◆ Brood cells

Description:

- ◆ It's where baby bees grow.
- ◆ They are different sizes for the different kinds of bees.
- ◆ The biggest ones are for new queen bees.
- ◆ Honeybees raise their young in the brood cells.
- ◆ Worker bees have the smallest brood cells.

Readers, we are noticing how writers use descriptive writing to give us information that will tell us more about their subjects. Knowing how descriptive writing can be used as a structure to help us make sense will make us more efficient readers.

Let's continue to explore how writers use this structure to help us read for meaning. As you move back to your space, take a book from the "All About" tub and explore how writers use descriptive writing to help us understand. I'll ask a few of you to share your findings at the end of our workshop today.

Flip It from Reading to Writing

As readers we come to recognize that writers often use description to open an idea or to draw the reader in. While we read we notice that description is one way a text can progress from one idea to the next. As writers we bring those details (or know how to access them) as we generate text. We layer in description that will help our readers gain deeper insight into our topic. In addition, writers need to understand when and where those additional details are needed by readers for support and elaboration.

▣ LESSON FOCUS Exploring Description as Writers

Writers, in our reading workshop we have been digging in to text structures and thinking about how writers organize their texts to help their readers make sense. Let's flip that idea over and think about how understanding text structure helps us as writers.

We learned how description is used as a structure to help us think about the text we are reading. We discovered the writer usually tells us the big idea, or subject, and then describes it with examples or explanations. Remember that we listed those when we explored the books about bees.

Now when we make a plan for our writing we can begin by thinking about the big ideas we need to include. I'm going to write about owls. Help me identify a few of the big ideas I will need to describe as I write. Take a moment now and turn to your partner and think of four big ideas I would need to include in my text. [Pause briefly as they collaborate to brainstorm the big ideas to include.]

Writers, I'd like to hear some of your thoughts. I'll jot them in my notebook as you share. [As you make notes, speak aloud what you are writing.]

- ◆ Owls are birds.
- ◆ Owl babies are hatched from eggs.
- ◆ Owls are nocturnal.
- ◆ Owls are predators.
- ◆ Owl pellets.

These big ideas can help me get organized. Let's review what I have written in my notebook. [Read each one from your notebook, and turn the notebook out to show students where you have written it.] I can write one paragraph on each big idea.

Now, let's remember what we noticed as readers. The writer tells us the big idea, or subject, and then uses description to give more information on each big idea. I think I will begin with the idea that owls are birds. I'm going to write that on the chart. [Turn to write this on the chart so they can see.]

The Subject:

- ◆ Owls are birds.

I will need to include examples or explanations or descriptions that will tell more about birds. Turn to your partner and think of three or four things I could add in this section. [Pause to let them talk.] Writers, let me hear some of your thoughts. I'll jot them in my notebook as I listen.

Description:

- ◆ Birds have feathers.

- Birds hatch from eggs.
- Some birds build nests for homes.
- Most birds can fly; owls can fly.
- Birds have beaks and use them to get food.

If I make a list like this for each of the big ideas you helped me think of, I will have a plan for my first draft. I'll get started on this today and show you my draft tomorrow.

Writers, I'll leave the chart to remind you how you can get organized for writing your "all about" book. Take a moment to list your topic at the top of a new page in your writer's notebook. [Pause a moment for them to write.] Now make a list of the big ideas you want to include in your book. If you get stuck you may want to think with your partner. [Pause briefly as they generate.] Let me hear from a few of you. [Speak into the work they have generated before sending them off to work.] Writers, when you are back in your spot, think about each big idea and jot down a few ideas you can add to explain or give examples in your description. Let's get started.

Writing Samples

These four samples show writers using description for different purposes beyond the development of an "all about" text. While Caleb's writing is similar to an "all about" format, it is more focused on a specific aspect of a game he enjoys (see Figure 1.1).

Abby uses description to bring the reader along on the search for the perfect hot pink bow (see Figure 1.2).

Trent uses description to zero in on the details needed to locate a lost jacket (see Figure 1.3).

Jinger uses description to elaborate and extend her personal narrative (see Figure 1.4).

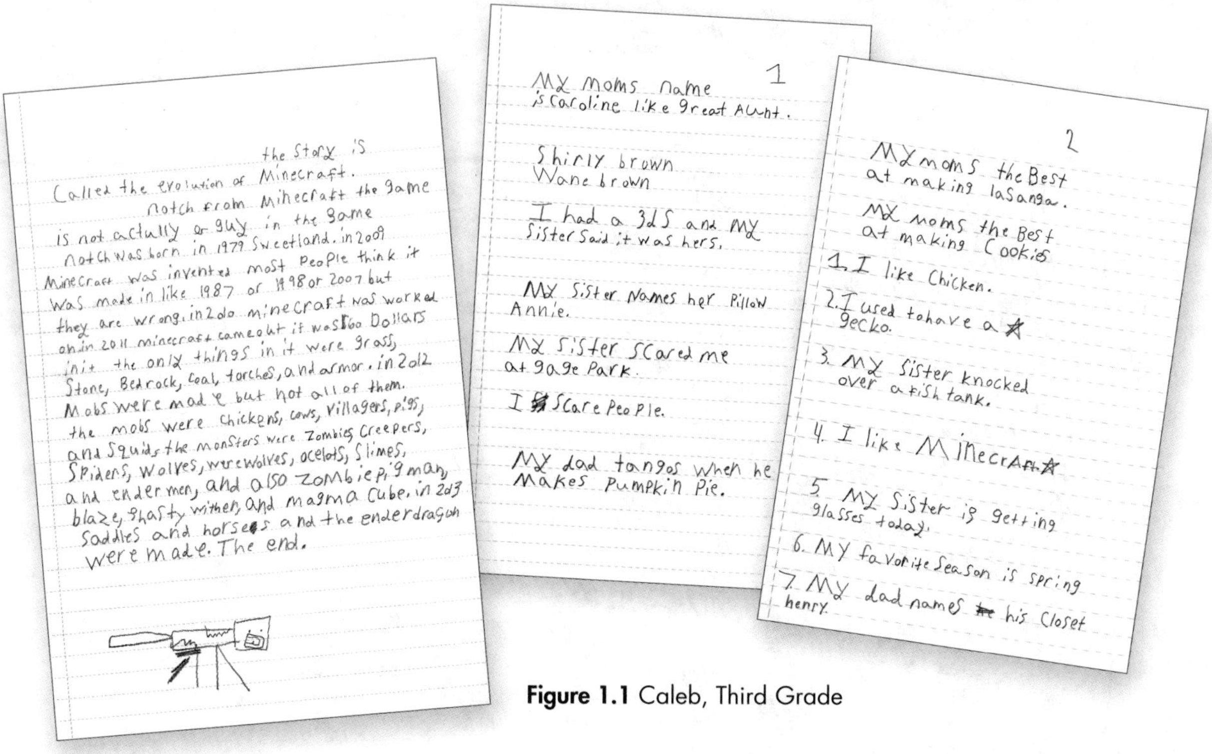

the story is
Called the evolution of Minecraft.
Notch from Minecraft the game
is not actually a guy in the game
Notch was born in 1979 Sweetland. in 2009
Minecraft was invented most People think it
was made in like 1987 or 1998 or 2007 but
they are wrong. in 2010 minecraft was worked
on in 2011 minecraft came out it was Too Dollars
in it the only things in it were grass,
Stone, Bedrock, Coal, torches, and armor. in 2012
Mobs were made but not all of them.
the mobs were chickens, cows, villagers, pigs,
and squids the monsters were Zombies Creepers,
Spiders, wolves, werewolves, ocelots, Slimes,
and endermen, and also zombie pigman,
blaze, ghasty wither, and magma Cube. in 2013
Saddles and horses and the enderdragon
were made. The end.

Figure 1.1 Caleb, Third Grade

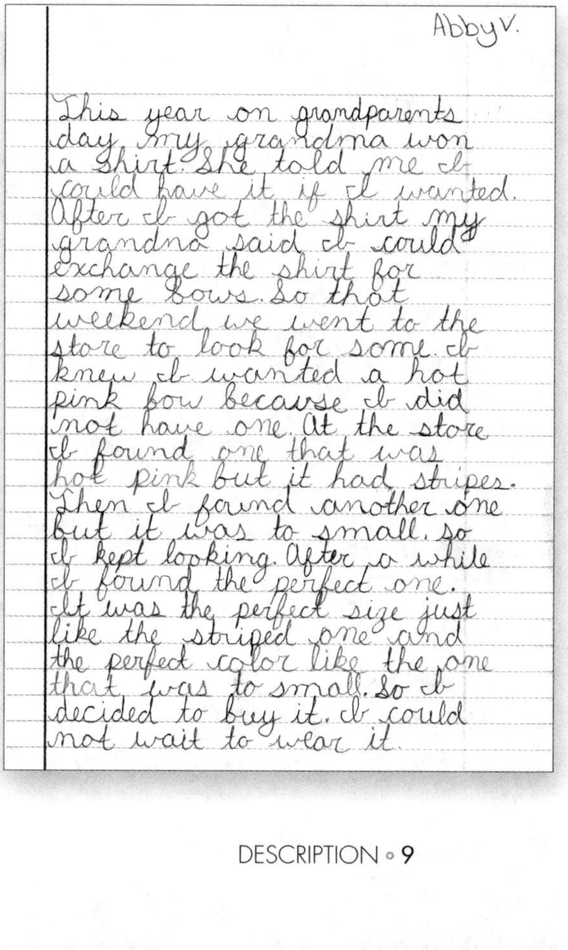

My moms name
is caroline like great Aunt.

Shirly brown
Wane brown

I had a 3dS and my
Sister said it was hers.

My Sister Names her Pillow
Annie.

My Sister Scared me
at gage Park.

I Scare People.

My dad tangos when he
Makes Pumpkin Pie.

My moms the Best
at making lasanga.

My moms the Best
at making Cookies

1. I like Chicken.

2. I used to have a gecko.

3. My Sister knocked
over a fish tank.

4. I like Minecraft

5. My Sister is getting
glasses today.

6. My favorite Season is spring.

7. My dad names his Closet
henry.

This year on grandparents
day my grandma won
a shirt. She told me I
could have it if I wanted.
After I got the shirt my
grandma said I could
exchange the shirt for
some bows. So that
weekend we went to the
store to look for some. I
knew I wanted a hot
pink bow because I did
not have one. At the store
I found one that was
hot pink but it had stripes.
Then I found another one
but it was to small. so
I kept looking. After a while
I found the perfect one.
It was the perfect size just
like the striped one and
the perfect color like the one
that was to small. So I
decided to buy it. I could
not wait to wear it.

Abby V.

Figure 1.2 Abby, Sixth Grade

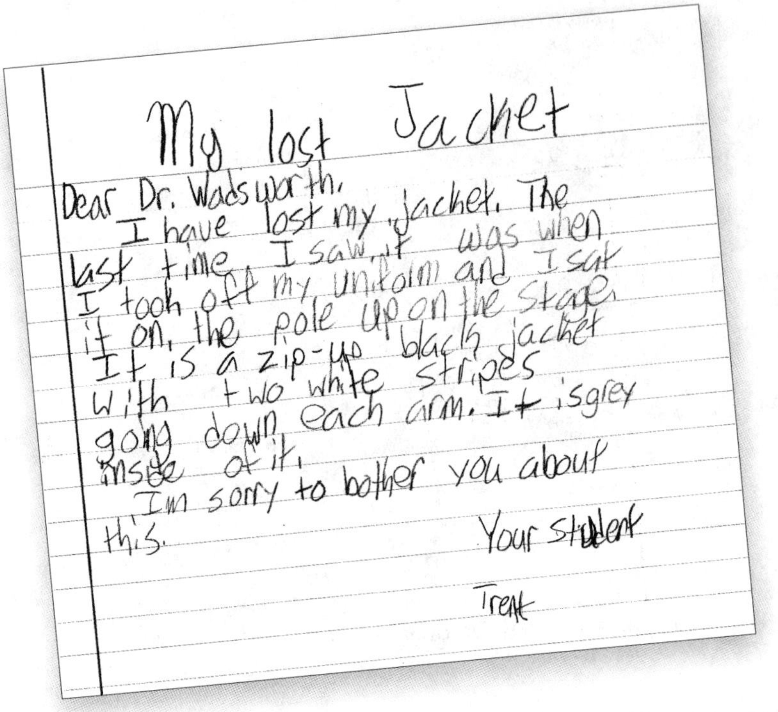

My lost Jacket

Dear Dr. Wadsworth,

I have lost my jacket. The last time I saw it was when I took off my uniform and I sat it on the pole up on the stage. It is a zip-up black jacket with two white stripes going down each arm. It is grey inside of it.

I'm sorry to bother you about this.

Your student

Trent

Figure 1.3 Trent, Fourth Grade

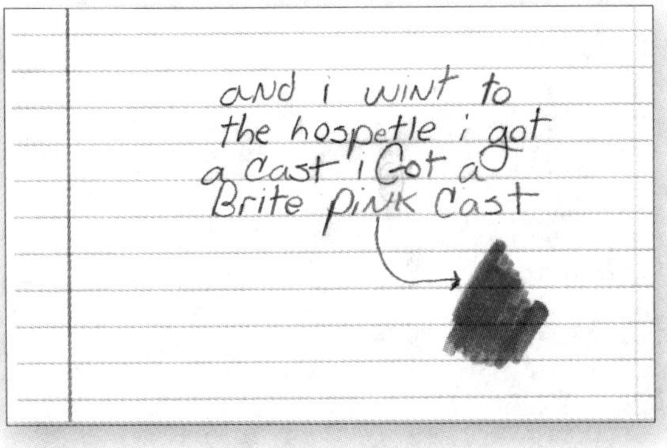

and i wint to the hospetle i got a cast i Got a Brite pink cast

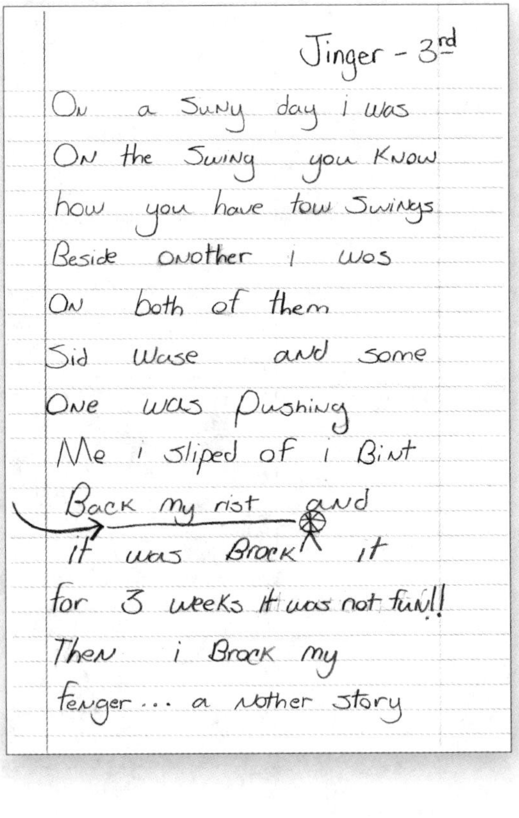

Figure 1.4 Jinger, Third Grade

Jinger - 3rd

On a Suny day I was
On the Swing you Know
how you have tou Swings
Beside onother I wos
On both of them
Sid Wase and some
One was Pushing
Me i sliped of i Bint
Back my rist and
it was Brock it
for 3 weeks it was not fun!!
Then i Brock my
fenger ... a nother story

Additional Texts: Description

Animals Nobody Loves by Seymour Simon: This nonfiction text uses rich description to present information about the subject. In each section, Simon describes, defines, and poses questions about each of the animals. Crisp photographs pair well with richly descriptive language.

Fireflies! by Julie Brinckloe: This short picture book focuses on a single summer evening spent catching fireflies and facing the dilemma of what to do with them. Each word is essential in this sparse text.

In November by Cynthia Rylant: The author uses many descriptive phrases, words, metaphors, and personification to help the reader understand November as she knows it (e.g., *In November, at winter's gate, the stars are brittle. The sun is a sometimes friend. And the world has tucked her children in, with a kiss on their heads, till spring.*).

Owl Moon by Jane Yolen: The author takes the reader owling on a snowy night to a place where trees stand still as giant statues. We walk with her over the crunchy snow-covered ground with only the bright moonlight to guide our steps. Yolen keeps the readers engaged with well-placed details on every page.

Twilight Comes Twice by Ralph Fletcher: The author uses rich description to paint a picture of very ordinary things that mark the arrival of dusk and dawn. He layers in additional detail to elaborate (e.g., *With invisible arms dawn erases the stars from the blackboard of night. Soon just the moon and a few stars remain.*).

2

SEQUENCE

Human beings like order. We sort things from large to small or dark to light and create order in our cabinets, drawers, and closets. We place books in alphabetical order on our bookshelves. Putting things in order helps us to find them and gives us a sense of comfort and control. One way we put things in order is by sequence. We organize our photos by the date they were taken or perhaps by location along the trip. We establish a sequence that makes sense for us. In our classrooms we begin working on sequence with our youngest students when we establish a routine for the day, as we introduce the schedule of events, or when we open the day with a morning circle that features the days of the week and months of the year. Sequence is a part of our lives from the start.

So it is no surprise that sequence is a familiar text structure in both fiction and nonfiction writing. Writers employ several ways of sequencing ideas, scenes, and events to organize their texts from beginning to end. Sequence, like other structures, helps the reader make sense of the writer's intentions and build meaning for himself.

Consider these possibilities for using sequence as a structure in writing:

Options for Sequence	Text Example
Alphabetical order	*ABCs of Baseball* by Peter Golenbock
Cumulative tale	*I Know an Old Lady Who Swallowed a Fly* by Mary Ann Hoberman

Options for Sequence	Text Example
Days of the week	*The Very Hungry Caterpillar* by Eric Carle
Diary entries by date	*Diary of a Spider* by Doreen Cronin
Event by event	*Henry's Freedom Box* by Ellen Levine
Generation by generation	*This Is the Rope* by Jacqueline Woodson
Life cycle	*Turtle Girl* by Carole Crowe
Location by location	*Locomotive* by Brian Floca
Months of the year	*A House for a Hermit Crab* by Eric Carle
Numbers	*Pumpkin Countdown* by Joan Holub (younger) *Just a Second* by Steve Jenkins (older)
Play by play	*Home Run: The Story of Babe Ruth* by Robert Burleigh
Recipe	*The Little Red Hen (Makes a Pizza)* by Philemon Sturges
Seasons	*City Dog, Country Frog* by Mo Willems
Signal words	*A Piece of Cake* by LeUyen Pham
Time of day	*The Napping House* by Audrey Wood
Timeline	*Franklin Roosevelt* by Judy Emerson (series with timelines)
Year by year	*Lady Liberty: A Biography* by Doreen Rappaport

◄❏ LESSON FOCUS Exploring Sequence as a Text Structure

R eaders, we have been exploring sequence as a text structure. Let's look again at the different ways authors can sequence their texts. [Refer to the charts where you are listing each structure as you introduce it. As these charts develop, they will become a known resource for student writers.]

Yesterday we read a stack of books and sorted them by the way the writer used sequence to organize the text. Later, during your partner reading time, I'd like you to continue to explore books in the sequence stack and add to the tubs we made yesterday. As you read with your partner decide which tub it belongs in. Place a sticky note on a page you can use as evidence for your decision.

Today let's take a look at a book from our sequence stack. [Hold up a copy of the book.] The title is *Alexander and the Terrible, Horrible, No Good, Very Bad Day* written by Judith Viorst. You'll remember that this story happens in just one day. A lot of things happened to Alexander in that one day. From the time he woke up in the morning to the time he went to bed, he had one thing after another happen to him. Judith Viorst must really know a lot about the things that can make a day rotten for a kid.

I'll read this story again today, and this time I want you to notice how Judith Viorst uses what she knows about a day in a kid's life to sequence the events. Think about the type of sequence she uses as her structure. Then we can decide which tub this book belongs in. [Read the book aloud. Pause at the end to give children time to reflect and think about the structure.]

Readers, let's take a look at the first page. Alexander is just waking up, and Judith Viorst writes about those things that happen in the morning when we get up.

- He went to sleep with gum in his mouth.
- He woke up with gum in his hair.
- He tripped on his skateboard when he got out of bed.
- He dropped his sweater in the sink while the water was running.

Judith Viorst tells us only things that happen when he is getting up. Notice she isn't telling about things that happen at lunch or at school. She will give us these details in the order they happen. She is using sequence. As I read the next page, notice what Judith Viorst chose to tell us about. [Read the page.]

Take a few seconds to think about how Judith Viorst uses what she knows about how things happen at certain times of the day and uses sequence as a structure on this page. [Pause briefly.] Readers, talk with your partner and share your thoughts about how this text structure worked to carry the story forward. [Pause briefly.] Let's hear from a few of you. What have you noticed about the use of sequence in this book? [Allow a few students to share their insights.]

Yes, she takes the next time of day and tells only what happens at that time. Let me summarize.

The next time of day is breakfast:

- ♦ Anthony found a toy car in his cereal box.

- ♦ Nick found a secret code ring in his cereal box.

- ♦ Alexander found cereal in his cereal box.

[Continue to move through a few more pages until they see the pattern of moving one step at a time through the day, and note how Judith Viorst pairs appropriate events with each segment of the day.]

Readers, we have identified a pattern here. Judith Viorst begins the text with Alexander waking up, then, having breakfast, and then riding in the carpool. When he arrives at school we move with him through his day. And in each segment of his day she includes events that would happen at that time.

As you move out to read on your own, continue to select books from the stack. While you read, remember to think about how the writer is using sequence to organize the text for you. Decide which tub the book would belong in. Place a sticky note on a page you can use as evidence for your decision.

⊟ LESSON FOCUS Exploring Sequence as a Text Structure in Reading

Readers, remember to bring your reading notebook and a pencil as we gather. [Allow time to gather.] Yesterday we explored Judith Viorst's book, *Alexander and the Terrible, Horrible, No Good, Very Bad Day*. We noticed that she organized the story by a sequence of events paired with the time of day those events happen. Today we are going to revisit another book from our sequence stack, *My Grandmother's Clock* by Geraldine McCaughrean. As we explore this text, focus on how this author gives several examples of using chronological order (sequence) to organize her writing for us.

As I read *My Grandmother's Clock* aloud I'd like you to make a list of the different examples she uses to show chronological order. [Read the book aloud. Keep the pacing slow so your students have time to think and jot down the examples they notice.] I'll pause here a moment and let you finish your lists. [Pause briefly.]

I noticed you found several examples of chronological order in this text. Geraldine McCaughrean is very clever. Let's take a moment now and revisit. As I turn each page I'll ask you to check your list and share the example you noticed there. I'll make a list of all your examples on the chart.

Seconds	[page 5]
Moments/Minutes	[page 6]
Hours	[page 6]
Day	[pages 10 and 12]
Days of the week	[pages 13 and 14]
Month	[page 15]
Seasons	[pages 17–21]
Year	[page 24]
Lifetime	[page 24]
Centuries	[page 26]

[List the examples they notice from each page and note the page number.]

Readers, do you notice a sequence here as well? [Pause briefly and let them think. Then, read the list aloud.] Notice how she begins with the smallest unit of time, seconds, then moves to the next larger unit of time, minutes, and to the next larger unit of time, hours, and so on until she ends with a very large unit of time, centuries. This is very interesting. Each example is one way to show chronological order. And the list is in chronological order. This one book has a lot of examples of using sequence to organize your writing for the reader.

I know you have been exploring books from the stack and sorting them into tubs. Think about the books you have read. Have you found a book where the writer uses more than one way to sequence? Take a moment to think about that today as you continue to explore how sequence is used to organize texts. If you find an example, place a sticky note on any pages you can use as evidence, and then leave the book in this tub. [Have an empty tub with you.] Remember, we will soon take these structures and flip them over to explore them in our writing.

Flip It from Reading to Writing

Readers rely on sequences to keep events organized in their minds and to understand how events and information are related within the text. Sequence offers logic and order as the reader weaves meaning. As writers we must recognize the various ways sequence can be used to present the information we intend our readers to acquire. Bringing a repertoire of sequencing options to our writing gives us flexibility in the delivery of our intentions.

W riters, we have been exploring structures and the different ways a writer can organize a text to help the reader make sense. The last structure we explored in our reading work was sequence. We identified several ways writers use sequence to organize their work. Today we are going to explore those ideas in our own writing. Let's begin with a quick review of what we discovered as readers. [Refer to the chart listing examples of sequence as a structure on page 16.]

When I write I usually choose something I know about, or something I really want to learn about. One thing all writers have to consider is how to organize what they write, even if it is something they know a lot about or something personal. Last night I wrote a short entry in my notebook about our time at school yesterday. I used sequence to organize my entry. As I read it aloud, I'd like you to identify which example of sequence I used.

Today we had an exciting day at school beginning with our Morning Message, which let us know we had a busy day ahead of us, filled with lots of activities. We had no idea how busy our day was really going to be! Right in the middle of reading the Morning Message, the fire alarm went off. We gathered and moved quickly from the building into the parking lot where we were greeted by a real fire truck with sirens blaring. Next, we learned that the alarm was for real (not just another fire drill) because there had been a fire in the cafeteria. Later that morning our principal came on the intercom and thanked us for being so well behaved during our two-hour (yes, two-hour) wait standing outside for the firemen to clear the building so we could return to our classroom. When we did finally return to our room, none of us could focus on our work so we spent the next two hours curled up all around the room reading and relaxing. I guess the fire alarm was a good thing after all.

Writers, I'll leave the example up on the screen for you to revisit as you take a moment to think about which example of sequence I used. Be sure to have your evidence ready. [Pause briefly as they get their thoughts together.] Now share your thoughts with your partner and point to the evidence from my entry. [Pause briefly.] Writers, let me hear from a few of you. [Allow three or four students to respond and offer examples from your entry.]

Yes, I did sequence my entry with examples from our day in the order they happened. And I used signal words to keep it moving forward. Let's quickly review those signal words I used.

- ◆ Beginning with
- ◆ Right in the middle
- ◆ Next

- ◆ Later in the morning
- ◆ Finally

I could have used a time sequence instead. If I had made that choice I would have written what time was on the clock when each event occurred. For example, I may have started like this:

> *Today turned out to be a very exciting day. It began like every other school day with the Morning Message at 8:00 a.m. But we didn't even finish the message because the fire alarm rang at 8:06 and we had to exit the building . . .*

Each time we write we are making decisions about how to organize. I want you to spend a few minutes with your notebooks and find two entries you could write from. Search for entries about ordinary events, things that have happened in your life. [Pause here briefly. Spend some time with your notebook as well, and have two examples ready to share.]

Writers, as we were searching I found these two possibilities. The first is an entry about washing my car last weekend. The second one is about going on a picnic with my friends last summer. Tell your partner the two possibilities you have found in your notebook. [Pause briefly.]

Writers, I believe everyone has two possibilities to work with. Now I want you to think about how you will sequence the events as you write. Revisit the examples from our list of ways to sequence, and select one to try as you tell your story. When you are ready to write give me a thumbs up. OK, off you go!

[Notice any writers who are hesitant to begin, and go to them first when beginning to confer. As you confer with other students, select a couple to share their thoughts in the after-workshop gathering.]

[At the end of writing time, give the signal to return to the carpet.]

Writers, I enjoyed seeing how you took what we learned as readers and flipped it over to use it in your writing today. I've asked a few of you to share what you did today. Let me hear from . . . [Ask those you tapped while conferring to comment on the sequence example they used and explain why they chose that one. If possible, project the piece of writing on the screen or whiteboard so you can point to the evidence in the writing.]

Writers, I see evidence that you are taking control of sequence. Tomorrow we will continue our work on this.

Writing Samples

Logan uses a chronological sequence to relay the events of a family story and a lesson learned (see Figure 2.1).

Steven uses sequence to bring us through the process of striking out, then hitting a home run (see Figure 2.2).

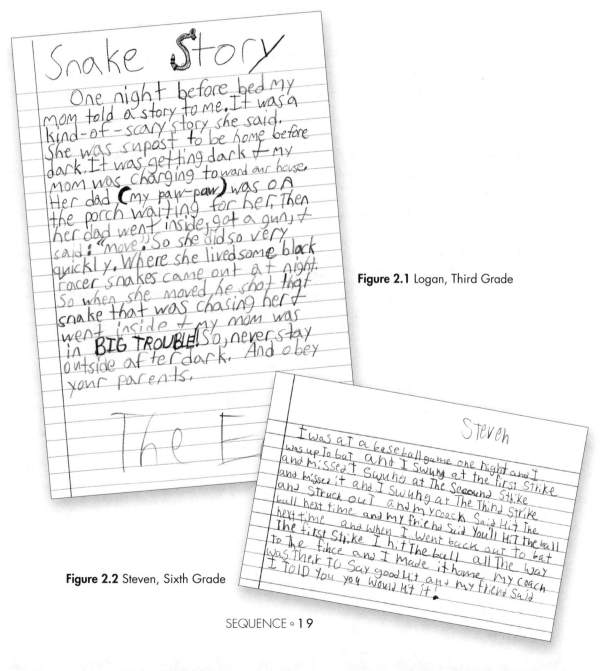

Figure 2.1 Logan, Third Grade

Figure 2.2 Steven, Sixth Grade

Additional Texts: Sequence

Brown Bear, Brown Bear, What Do You See? by Bill Martin, Jr.: This familiar book uses repeated words in a pattern to introduce young children to various animals to show sequencing. The pattern is broken when Martin introduces the teacher who sees the children who in turn sees all the animals in a review on the last spread.

Seven Blind Mice by Ed Young: The text uses ordinal numbers (on the first day . . . on the second day . . .) to move the reader from beginning to end as seven blind mice (each a different color) investigate the various parts of an elephant. It culminates with the final mouse (white mouse) synthesizing all the information to determine that the new something is an elephant.

The Very Hungry Caterpillar by Eric Carle: This text is organized using days of the week and number (cultural sequences). The caterpillar begins eating on Sunday and continues through the days of the week. Each day he increases the number of items he eats by one. By the end of the week he builds a cocoon and emerges as a butterfly.

What Did You Do Today? by Toby Forward: This book takes the reader through the school day in a logical event-by-event sequence. The short text moves from the beginning of the school day to the ending. A mirror sequence is revealed on the opposite page showing the mother's day from the beginning of the day to the end.

3

PROBLEM AND SOLUTION

The problem/solution structure, a typical feature in story and fiction, presents a problem or obstacle near the beginning of the text. As the story unfolds the character works to face or overcome the obstacle, and the problem is usually solved by the end of the story. This structure may be seen as the overarching framework for a persuasive essay where the writer intends to persuade the reader to endorse a particular idea or action. In this case, the reader would need to identify the problem or concern in the opening segment (the city wants to close a park to erect a building), note the argument presented as a solution (save the park and construct the building in another part of the city), and then decide whether to accept, question, or reject the ideas presented. A problem/solution structure may also be found in an essay where the writer identifies a common problem (finding a parking place) followed by suggestions to solve the problem (walk, ride a bike, take a taxi).

⊷ LESSON FOCUS Introduce Problem and Solution as a Text Structure

Today we are going to think about a structure called problem and solution. When a writer uses this structure to organize a story, you will meet a character with a problem near the beginning. As you keep reading you find out how the character's problem gets solved. So there's a clear problem and a solution for the problem.

Here's a story we have read before just for fun, *Click, Clack, Moo: Cows That Type* by Doreen Cronin. This story is a clear example of a problem/solution structure because we can see the problem on the first page; let's take a look.

In the first sentence we find out which character has a problem, and we find out what his problem is. Listen as I read that page: "Farmer Brown has a problem. His cows like to type. All day long he hears click, clack, moo. Click, clack, moo. Click, clack, moo." You may remember Farmer Brown doesn't like hearing the typewriter click-clack all day long. When he asked the cows to stop, they asked for electric blankets because the barn was cold at night.

When a writer uses a problem/solution structure, the reader finds the problem near the beginning. If you want to find out how the character solves the problem you have to keep reading and thinking. As you read you ask yourself, "How is this helping the character solve the problem?"

- Which character had a problem?

  – Farmer Brown

- What problem did the character have?

  – His cows made too much noise typing, and they wanted electric blankets.

- What steps did the character take trying to solve the problem?

  – He told them no blankets.

  – They said no milk then.

  – And the hens said no eggs.

  – The cows agreed to trade the typewriter for the electric blankets.

- What solution finally solved the problem?

  – Farmer Brown agreed to give them the electric blankets.

When a text, like this story, presents the problem clearly in the beginning, we expect to find out how the problem gets solved. So we read to find out what the solution is going to be. In *Click, Clack, Moo: Cows That Type*, we find out the solution is that Farmer Brown finally gets electric blankets for the cows and they give up the typewriter.

Let's make a note about what we remember here.

⬅️ LESSON FOCUS Exploring Problem and Solution as a Text Structure

R eaders, we have been digging in to structure and looking for the ways writers organize their texts to help us make sense of what we read. Recently we revisited *Click, Clack, Moo: Cows That Type* and found the problem and the solution in that book.

Remember, in fiction the character usually has some obstacle or problem to deal with. And usually the reader finds the solution by the end of the story. In *Click, Clack, Moo: Cows That Type* the author tells us the character's problem in the first sentence: "Farmer Brown has a problem. His cows like to type." But some books don't tell us so clearly.

Let's think about a book we read yesterday. I asked you to think about three things before I read *Trevor's Wiggly-Wobbly Tooth* by Lester Laminack aloud:

1. Which character has a problem?

2. What is the problem?

3. What is the solution that solves the problem?

We decided that Trevor is the character with a problem. We were expecting that from the title, *Trevor's Wiggly-Wobbly Tooth,* and we predicted that his problem would have something to do with his tooth. Sometimes the title will give us a hint.

After we read the story we decided Trevor's problem was that he wanted to lose a tooth because he was the only one in his class without a missing-tooth smile. But, he was a little nervous about it. And we noticed even though he worried about a lot of possibilities, the solution to his problem was the taffy that his Grandma Sally made at school.

Today, I'm going to read parts of *Trevor's Wiggly-Wobbly Tooth* again, and I'd like you to be thinking about how the author lets us know what the problem is. I'll read the first few pages and pause for you to think and talk with your partner. [Read the first three pages aloud.] We know who the character is, and we know what problem he is facing. Think about how the author let us know that. [Sit quietly and think and make a few notes.]

Would you turn now to your partner and tell what you were thinking about. [Pause briefly.] Readers, let's pause our conversations. I'd like to hear your thoughts. [Allow a few to share their insights, and then summarize to answer the question you posed.]

So it seems most of us agree the author let us know about the problem when he said, "Everyone in Mr. Thompson's class had a missing-tooth smile. Everyone except Trevor." And a little more when he said, "Trevor began to worry."

In *Click, Clack, Moo: Cows That Type* the author just told us: "Farmer Brown has a problem." But in *Trevor's Wiggly-Wobbly Tooth*, the author doesn't just say Trevor has a problem. We know that wanting to lose a tooth is a problem because he is the last one in his class and he is beginning to worry about it.

Readers, let's make a question out of his problem and see if that will help us think about the story in a new way. Like this, we know Trevor's problem is that he wants to lose a tooth, but he is worried about it. So I'll ask myself this question: "How will he get that wiggly tooth out?" I know if I keep reading and thinking about that question, I will be looking for the solution, just like Trevor. When you find a book with a problem/solution structure you could try to make a question out of the problem. That may help you think about the story in a new way.

Flip It from Reading to Writing

Understanding a problem/solution structure as readers gives us focus. As we identify the problem, whether in a persuasive essay, a feature article, or the plot of a story, our minds begin attending to details in search of possible solutions. As writers we flip that insight. We know the solution we plan to offer and present the problem early in the text to draw the reader in. Knowing the solution gives us a focal point, an ending to work toward as we generate text.

▶ LESSON FOCUS Exploring Problem and Solution in Writing

Writers, in our reading workshop we have been digging in to text structures and thinking about how writers organize their texts to help their readers make sense. Let's flip that idea over and think about how understanding text structure helps us as writers.

We learned how a problem/solution structure helps us think about the text we are reading. We discovered asking the following three questions helped us focus as we read:

1. Who has a problem?

2. What is the problem?

3. How does it get solved?

Now when we begin making a plan for our writing, we can ask those same questions.

Help me think about that for a story I am planning to write. I'm going to write about the time I went to the grocery store and locked my keys in the car.

Let's think about the first two questions to get my thoughts organized for writing today.

1. Who has a problem?

2. What is the problem?

[Pause briefly.]

Writers, share your thoughts with your partner.

[Pause briefly.]

Now let me hear from a few of you. What did you come up with?

[Make note of responses.]

Let's begin with the first question. Who has a problem?

That was easy wasn't it? It's me; I am the character with the problem in this story. We all agree on that.

What is the problem?

Exactly, I locked my keys in my car. So now I can't get in the car to drive home.

As I plan my writing for today I have two questions answered. I know that I'm the character with a problem, and I know the problem is my keys are locked inside my car.

Now let's think about the third question we consider when thinking about a problem/ solution structure. How will the problem get solved?

Remember when we were reading we tried turning the problem into a question. Let's try that as we think like writers. The problem is that I locked my keys in the car. If we make a question out of my problem we could ask: "How will I get my keys out of that locked car?"

Think for a few seconds, then list at least two things I could try to solve this problem.

[Pause briefly.]

Share your ideas with your partner and stretch your lists.

[Pause briefly.]

Let's hear some of your thoughts.

[Make note of ideas as they share.]

Writers, we have several ideas listed. As I read through the list let's think about which of these are things I might actually try.

- Find the police.
- Ask someone on the street to help.
- Break the window.
- Call the car company.
- Call a locksmith.
- Ask the people in the grocery store if anyone knows how to unlock a car.
- Call your dad.

You have helped me think of several ways I can solve the problem when I write the story. And, of course, I do know how I finally got my car unlocked. But I'll save that detail for the end of the story. You'll have to read it to find out.

So, writers, how will I use your suggestions? Think like a reader for a moment. When we are reading a story with a problem/solution structure, we do not usually find the solution right away. Reflect on how Doreen Cronin revealed Farmer Brown's problem in *Click, Clack, Moo: Cows That Type*. He had cows that typed all day, and he didn't like to hear the noise. We know that he gave the cows electric blankets in exchange for that typewriter. But we know that he tried several other things first. And in *Trevor's Wiggly-Wobbly Tooth*, Lester Laminack showed us that Trevor was the only kid in first grade without a missing tooth and he wanted to lose a tooth. We know that on Friday his tooth came out in the taffy, but he thought about and worried over several other ways to get that tooth out.

When I write the story I need to build tension and make the character struggle a bit to solve this problem. It shouldn't be too easy. So I think I'll have him try a couple of the things on your list before he comes up with the one that solves his problem. Now I'm ready to get started.

Today as you move out to work on your stories try to begin with answering those three questions:

1. Who has a problem?

2. What is the problem?

3. What are the ways it could be solved?

Writing Samples

Taylor uses the problem/solution structure to let readers know about how she lost and later found her dog (see Figure 3.1).

Angelina opens with a problem clearly defined. She takes action, and the problem is solved when the teacher tells two girls to pull their cards (see Figure 3.2).

Caden introduces the problem of a ball accidently going into the water and explores the options before making a decision (see Figure 3.3).

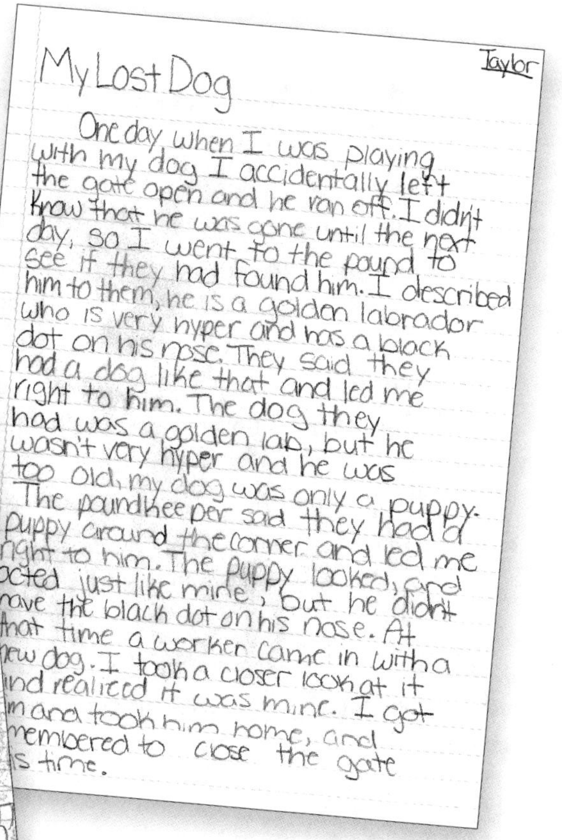

Figure 3.1 Taylor, Fifth Grade

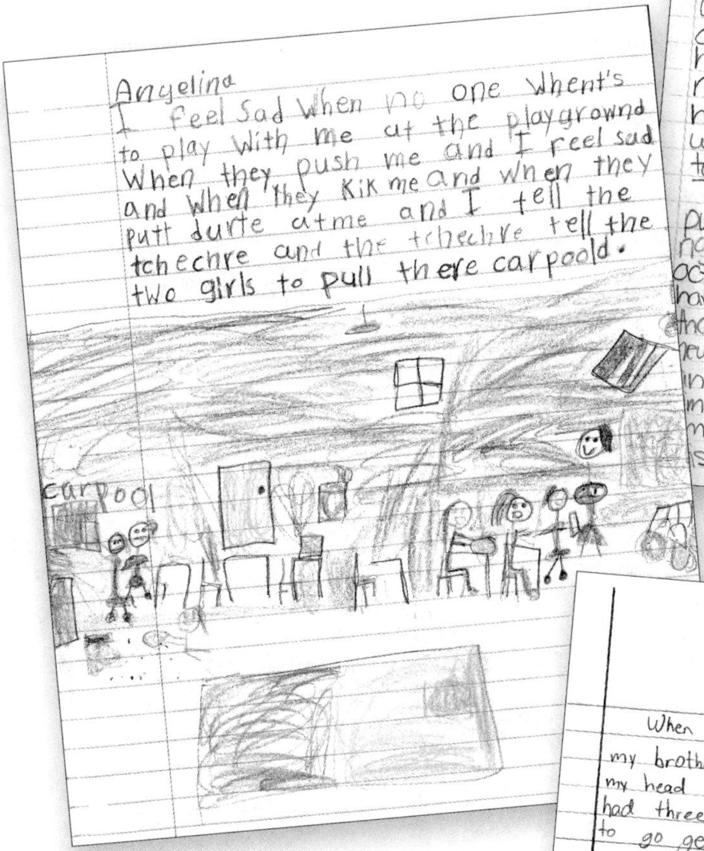

Taylor

My Lost Dog

One day when I was playing with my dog I accidentally left the gate open and he ran off. I didn't know that he was gone until the next day, so I went to the pound to see if they had found him. I described him to them, he is a golden labrador who is very hyper and has a black dot on his nose. They said they had a dog like that and led me right to him. The dog they had was a golden lab, but he wasn't very hyper and he was too old, my dog was only a puppy. The poundkeeper said they had a puppy around the corner and led me right to him. The puppy looked and acted just like mine, but he didn't have the black dot on his nose. At that time a worker came in with a new dog. I took a closer look at it and realized it was mine. I got him and took him home, and remembered to close the gate this time.

Angelina

I feel sad when no one whent's to play with me at the playground and when they push me and I feel sad when they kik me and when they putt durte at me and I tell the tchechre and the tchechre tell the two girls to pull there carpoold.

carpool

Figure 3.2 Angelina, First Grade
(ELL student)

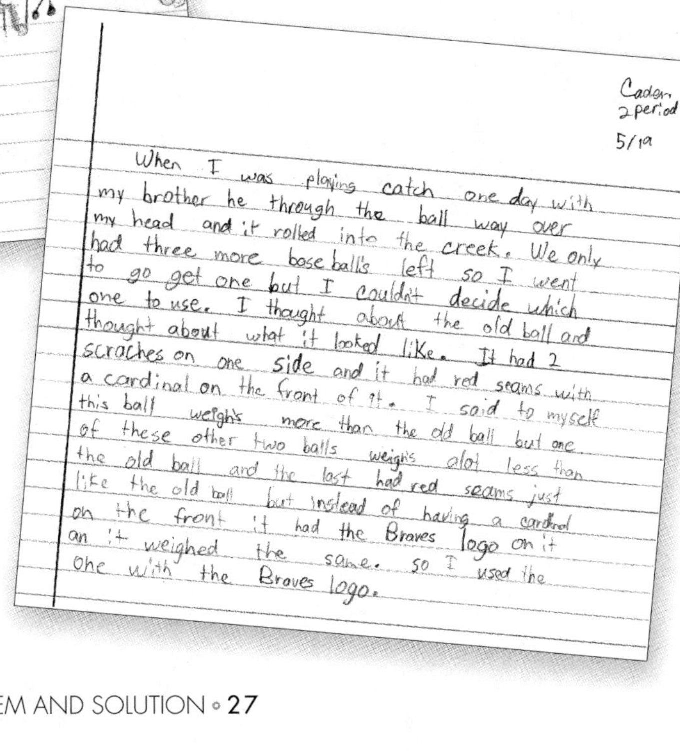

Figure 3.3 Caden, Fifth Grade

Caden
2 period
5/19

When I was playing catch one day with my brother he through the ball way over my head and it rolled into the creek. We only had three more base balls left so I went to go get one but I couldn't decide which one to use. I thought about the old ball and thought about what it looked like. It had 2 scraches on one side and it had red seams with a cardinal on the front of it. I said to myself this ball weighs more than the old ball but one of these other two balls weighs alot less than the old ball and the last had red seams just like the old ball but instead of having a cardinal on the front it had the Braves logo on it an it weighed the same. So I used the one with the Braves logo.

Additional Texts: Problem and Solution

Baseball Saved Us by Ken Mochizuki: This story takes place during World War II when many Japanese Americans were placed into internment camps in the United States. To relieve their boredom and sadness, the people form a baseball team.

Chrysanthemum by Kevin Henkes: The problem in this story is that Chrysanthemum comes to dislike her name. A series of events across the story lead us to meet her music teacher who also has a flower name and the problem is solved.

Knuffle Bunny: A Cautionary Tale by Mo Willems: The problem occurs when Trixie and her dad realize they have left Trixie's beloved bunny at the laundromat. The solution is reached when they retrace their steps (sequencing) across town to find the missing bunny.

Mr. George Baker by Amy Hest: Mr. George is 100 years old and can't read. He goes back to elementary school with his young neighbor to learn how to read.

4

COMPARE AND CONTRAST

H ow often have you heard children say something like: "I have that exact same shirt, but mine is green stripes, not blue." Or, "I like your pink book bag. Mine is pink too, but yours has two pockets for pencils and stuff. Mine doesn't have any pockets on the outside. I wish it did." Perhaps noting similarities and differences is one of the ways we make sense of our world and communicate our wants and needs more clearly. This early sort of comparing and contrasting could be tapped as a gateway to helping readers and writers understand how this text structure helps to organize our thinking and facilitate our understanding.

Learning to distinguish similarities and differences is a necessary part of this structure, but learning to communicate those similarities and differences is a step toward controlling this structure both as a reader and as a writer.

When using a compare/contrast structure, writers often signal comparison by using words such as these:

- ✦ similar to
- ✦ alike
- ✦ same as
- ✦ also

- not only _____ , but also _____
- too
- like
- much as
- similarly
- both

When using a compare/contrast structure, writers often signal contrast by using words such as these:

- more than
- less than
- on the contrary
- on the other hand
- although
- however
- whereas
- different from

⊞ LESSON FOCUS   Introduce the Compare/Contrast Structure

Readers, we are continuing to explore text structures to learn how writers organize their texts to help us make sense when we read. Today we are going to explore a structure called compare and contrast. We compare and contrast things almost every day. For example, we are comparing when we say, "Our backpacks are so much alike. Both of them have a pocket on the side for a water bottle. The zipper pull on yours is the same as the zipper pull on mine. The color and pattern are the same, too." We are comparing when we notice and explain how two or more things are alike.

But, when we notice and explain how two or more things are different, that is called contrasting. Here's an example of what we might say if were noting contrast: "Our backpacks are almost the same, but mine is different from yours because yours has three small pockets on the front, whereas mine has only one large pocket. However, on the inside of the big pocket on my backpack there are little slots for pencils and a phone."

Today we are going to examine the compare/contrast structure in a nonfiction book, *Brown Bear or Black Bear?* by Heather Warren and Robbie Byerly. This book uses compare and contrast to help us identify brown bears and black bears. It shows us how they are alike and how they are different. It's very short so I'll read it once all the way through. I'll go slowly and pause so we can notice details in the photographs. Your job is to notice the ways these two bears are the same and the ways they are different from each other.

[Read the book aloud. Read at a slow pace, allowing time to connect the text to the details being featured in the photographs.]

Readers, sit with your ideas for a few seconds, and think about how these two bears are different from each other.

[Pause briefly.]

Tell your partner three ways the brown bear and the black bear are different from each other.

[Pause.]

Readers, I have my notebook open and ready to write. Let me hear from a few of you. Tell me something your partner noticed.

[Make a list in your notebook as students offer points of contrast between the brown bear and the black bear.]

Let's take a moment to check my list as I read it back to you.

[Read the list.]

Now let's think about how brown bears and black bears are alike. Sit with your thoughts for a few seconds. Think about what we learned from reading this book.

[Pause briefly.]

Tell your partner three ways the brown bear and the black bear are alike.

[Pause briefly.]

Readers, I have my notebook open and ready to write. Let me hear from a few of you. Tell me something your partner noticed.

[Make a list in your notebook as students offer points of comparison between the brown bear and the black bear.]

Let's take a moment to check my list as I read it back to you.

[Read the list of students' comments.]

Readers, these two writers used a compare/contrast structure to help us learn more about brown bears and black bears. I'm going to take what we noticed and make a chart. As you go back to your reading, be observant. The writer may be using compare and contrast to help you learn more about your topic as well.

[Before the next gathering use your notes to create a chart featuring the points of comparison and contrast. Incorporate the use of signal words when appropriate. You may find it helpful to use two colors, for example, contrast in red and compare in blue. It may look something like Figure 4.1.]

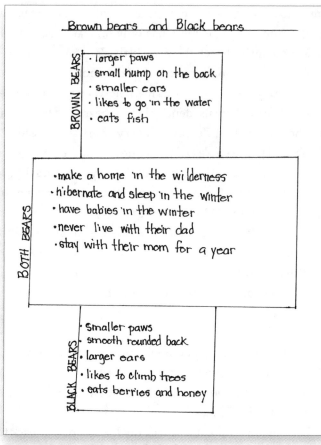

Figure 4.1 Brown Bears and Black Bears Chart

◄▢ LESSON FOCUS Exploring the Compare/Contrast Structure

Readers, yesterday we explored how authors can use the compare/contrast structure to help the reader learn new information. The authors of our book, *Brown Bear or Black Bear?*, used compare and contrast to help us learn how to identify which bear is a brown bear and which is a black bear. I took our noticings from yesterday and made a chart. Let's take a look.

[Review the chart.]

In these comments we are showing how the two bears are different. We are showing the contrast between them. That information will help us identify each of the two bears.

Notice the words writers use when showing contrast.

[Introduce the signal words for contrast here.]

Brown bears and black bears are different from each other in these ways:

- Brown bears *are larger than* black bears.
- Brown bears are about four feet high *whereas* black bears are about two and one-half feet high.
- A brown bear has a small hump on its back; *however*, the black bear has a smooth, rounded back.
- Brown bears have *smaller* ears *than* the black bear.
- Brown bears have *larger* paws *than* the black bear.
- Brown bears like to eat fish; *on the contrary*, black bears eat berries and honey.
- Brown bears like to go in the water; *however*, black bears like to climb trees.

In these comments we are showing how the two bears are alike. We are comparing them. This information helps us to notice all the features they share as bears. Notice the words writers use when showing similarities.

[Introduce the signal words for comparison here.]

Brown bears and black bears are alike in these ways:

- *Both* brown bears *and* black bears make a home in the wilderness.
- Brown bears hibernate *the same as* black bears. *Both* types of bears sleep in winter.
- Brown bears, *like* black bears, have babies in the winter.
- *Neither* brown bear babies nor black bear babies live with their dad.
- *Just like* baby brown bears, baby black bears live with their mom for over a year.

I'll leave this chart up for you to refer to as we continue our study of text structures.

Readers, today we are going to explore another nonfiction book. You may remember this book from our shark study. The title is *Who Would Win? Killer Whale vs. Great White Shark.* The author is Jerry Pallotta. This book has much more information than the book we read yesterday.

[Open the book to pages 6 and 7 where the focus is teeth.]

In this book Jerry Pallotta uses a compare/contrast structure to help us understand the differences between the killer whale and the great white shark. The left page gives us information about the killer whale, and the right page gives us information about the great white shark. Jerry Pallotta uses that format all the way through the book.

I'll use that format to make a chart that will help us keep track of our thinking.

[Turn to the chart and draw a line down the center. Label the left column Killer Whale. Label the right column Great White Shark.]

Since we have read this book for science, I'm going to select only a few pages for us to explore. Today our job is to notice how using compare and contrast can help us learn about the killer whale and the great white shark.

I'll read a couple of pages and pause for us to think about the ways these two creatures are alike and how they are different.

[Read pages 6 and 7.]

The focus of these two pages is teeth. Sit with this information for a few seconds, and think about how the teeth of the killer whale are different from or like the teeth of the great white shark.

[Pause briefly.]

Talk with your partner and share your information.

[Pause briefly.]

Readers, let's get some of the information on our chart. I need a few of you to share something your partner helped you think of.

[Record their comments on the chart.]

Let's take a look at another page.

[Turn to pages 10 and 11.]

Killer Whale	Great White Shark
• Teeth are smooth and look sort of like a finger.	• Teeth are triangle shaped.
• Teeth are about four inches long.	• Teeth are very sharp.
• Teeth are pointed on one end.	• The edges are like a saw.
• Have about fifty teeth.	• If a tooth comes out, it will grow back.
• If a tooth comes out, it doesn't grow back.	• It can lose more than 3,000 teeth.

I'll read these two pages and pause for us to think about the ways these two creatures are alike and how they are different.

[Read pages 10 and 11.]

The focus of these pages is food source or prey. Sit with this information for a few seconds, and think about how the food source of the killer whale is similar to or different from the food source of the great white shark.

[Pause briefly.]

Talk with your partner and share your information.

[Pause briefly.]

Readers, let's get some of the information on our chart. I need a few of you to share something your partner helped you think of.

[Record their comments on the chart.]

Killer Whale	Great White Shark
• Is a meat eater.	• Is a fish eater.
• Seals and sea lions are their favorite.	• Have been know to eat seal, sea lions, and even sea turtles.
• Also eat salmon and other fish.	• They would eat a person.
• King of the food chain.	• Is high on the food chain.
• Has no natural enemies.	• Largest predatory fish.

I will leave this book here on the counter for anyone who would like to continue exploring this structure.

⬅ LESSON FOCUS Exploring the Compare/Contrast Structure

Readers, today we are going to explore how a writer uses compare and contrast in fiction. We are going to revisit a book we have shared as a read-aloud, *First Grade Stinks!*, by Mary Ann Rodman.

You'll remember in this story Haley is excited about first grade until she finds out how different it is from kindergarten. As the story unfolds we see how Mary Ann Rodman uses compare and contrast to let us know what Haley is thinking about kindergarten and first grade.

- Miss Lacy's shirt is the color of daffodils with matching sneakers, but Ms. Gray's shirt is the color of dead leaves, and she has ugly brown sandals.

- The kindergarten room has a dragon kite hanging and leaf cutouts on the walls whereas the first-grade room has nothing hanging from the ceiling and nothing on the walls.

I'll read and pause a few times so we can explore how the writer uses compare and contrast to help us understand how Haley adjusts to being a first grader.

[Read the first two spreads aloud.]

Readers, in these first few pages we can see Mary Ann Rodman using compare and contrast to let us know how Haley is thinking and feeling about her new classroom and teacher. Take just a few seconds to recall what Haley says to contrast her new first-grade classroom and teacher with her classroom and teacher from kindergarten.

[Pause briefly.]

I'll make notes on the chart as you recall the ways they are different. Let's hear from a few of you.

[Allow time for a few students to share their insights as you jot them on the chart.]

I'm going to read a few more pages. As you listen notice how first grade is different from their kindergarten class.

[Read to the scene where the class is at lunch.]

Readers, in these pages we can see Mary Ann Rodman using compare and contrast to let us know how Haley is thinking and feeling about the differences between first grade and kindergarten. Take just a few seconds to recall what Haley says to contrast the two.

[Pause briefly.]

I'll add to our chart as you recall the ways they are different. Let's hear from a few of you:

- The day starts with work in first grade, but kindergarten starts with share time.

- In first grade, Ryan hands out the writing paper, whereas in kindergarten, Haley always handed out the paper.

- In kindergarten they had two recesses, yet there is only one recess in first grade.

Readers, remember as the story continues Haley notices a few more differences between kindergarten and first grade. She continues to say, "first grade stinks." At the end she changes her mind when she finds out there is no naptime in first grade. That's a difference she likes about first grade. So, we can see that Mary Ann Rodman is using compare and contrast to help us understand how Haley is feeling.

Readers, now we've explored both nonfiction and fiction texts that use compare and contrast to help us understand. We noticed several different ways writers can use compare and contrast, and we've created charts to help us remember what we noticed. Tomorrow we are going to explore a stack of books with our partners. I'll ask you to use a sticky note to mark a page where you find evidence of compare and contrast. And I'd like to hear your thoughts about how it helps you make sense of what you are reading.

Flip It from Reading to Writing

When we are reading, the compare/contrast structure helps us to deepen our understanding by highlighting similarities and differences among and between two or more things. Being able to think of a new idea in relation to other more familiar notions can be helpful. When we flip those insights into our writing work, we must be the bearer of the information and knowledge. As writers we have the responsibility of presenting new information to our readers. Having access to this structure provides a format for helping our readers weave meaning from the threads of our knowledge with their own.

✦ LESSON FOCUS Writing with Signal Words to Show Compare and Contrast

Writers, in our reading work we have recently explored how compare and contrast can help us learn about a topic or understand how someone is thinking or feeling. We discovered several ways a writer can use compare and contrast to organize texts. Finding the best way to organize our writing helps the reader understand our thoughts.

We discovered that writers use compare and contrast when they want to show how two or more things are alike or different. We began our study of compare and contrast with a very simple book about brown bears and black bears. After reading the book you shared what you learned, and I made a list of information in my notebook. Later, I made a chart to help us remember how the two bears compare and contrast.

[Show the chart using signal words to compare and contrast brown bears and black bears, page 33.]

Writers often use signal words to alert the reader when they are going to compare or contrast two or more things. Let's review those words and note how they help our readers understand. This chart shows the words writers use to signal similarities (compare) and differences (contrast).

Take a moment to review those signal words. Read through the chart, and look for the words that signal the spots where I compare or contrast the information we learned from the book.

[Pause briefly.]

Writers, talk with your partners, and identify the signal words in each statement.

[Pause briefly.]

Let's return to our chart. Writers, take a look at the statements here. Let's highlight the words that signal we are going to compare or contrast information.

[Read through each statement, and highlight the signal words as partners identify them.]

Let's write a few compare or contrast statements using these signal words. I have the chart with the information we took from reading Jerry Pallotta's book about the killer whale and great white shark.

[Show the charts listing information about the teeth and food sources of killer whales and great white sharks, pages 34 and 35.]

This chart is a list of facts. I would like you and your partner to use this information and our signal words to write three statements that compare and contrast the killer whale and the great white shark.

[Allow time for partners to draft their statements.]

Writers, I'd like to hear a few of your statements. When you share one, please tell us the signal words you selected and why you chose them.

[Take note of the level of understanding.]

Writers, we will continue working with compare and contrast, and soon we will use this structure in our nonfiction writing. Today as you go back to your writing, consider what you want your reader to know, and think about the best structure to help them understand. OK, writers, time to write.

W riters, let's review what we have learned about compare and contrast. Here is the chart from our work with *First Grade Stinks!* Take a moment and think about how Mary Ann Rodman used compare and contrast to help us understand how Haley was feeling about her first day in first grade.

[Review the chart to make sure writers understand the pattern. Invite comments, but keep it brief. See the chart on page 36.]

We've noticed that each time Haley experiences something new in first grade, she thinks about how it was different in kindergarten. Mary Ann Rodman shows us the contrast between Haley's feelings about first grade and kindergarten.

So, today let's try this in our writing. I'll try it out and you listen. When I'm trying something new in my writing, it is easier for me if I write about something I know really well. I'll write about what happened to me on Monday afternoon. I'll write this in the air so you can hear. Then, I'll write in my notebook when we move to our writing spots:

> *On Monday after school I dropped my favorite pen, and it rolled into the storm drain. I decided to stop on the way home to buy a new one. When I got in the store I walked to the aisle where all the pens are, but they didn't have any more like the one I lost. I thought about my old pen and all the things I liked about it. Then I started searching for a new pen. The first one I picked up was blue just like my old one, but it was a roller ball with liquid ink. I don't like liquid ink because I'm left handed and it smears on my hand when I write. My old pen had gel ink. I like gel ink best of all. The second one I picked up had gel ink just like my old one, but it was really thin and very short. I could barely hold it in my hand. My old pen fit just right in my hand. Then, I saw a pen that looked almost like my old pen. It was blue, just like my old pen. It had gel ink like my old pen, too. The only difference was the new pen had stripes on it. I like stripes, so I decided to give it a try.*

Writers, I'd like you to try using compare and contrast in a personal narrative. Take a few minutes to think or read through your notebook and find an event you could write about today.

[Allow time to generate the topic.]

When you have your idea, let me see a thumbs up.

[Note who may be struggling with topic selection.]

OK, writers, let's get started.

[Remember that new moves in writing make take several attempts. Be patient and supportive.]

Writing Samples

Maddux uses a compare/contrast structure to explain the difference between Minor A baseball and Ozone baseball (see Figure 4.2).

Jake uses compare and contrast to give his readers an insider view of the process he went through when choosing a new dog (see Figure 4.3).

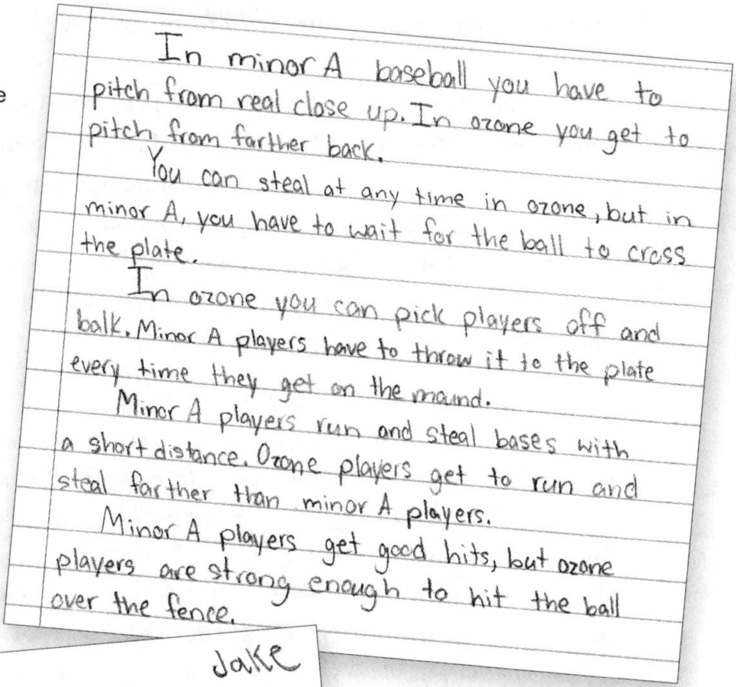

Figure 4.2 Maddux, Fifth Grade

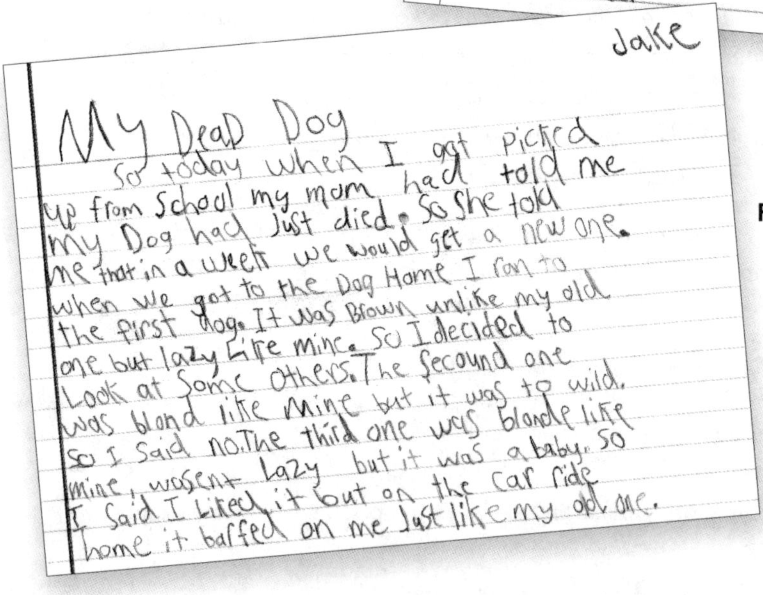

> In minor A baseball you have to pitch from real close up. In ozone you get to pitch from farther back.
>
> You can steal at any time in ozone, but in minor A, you have to wait for the ball to cross the plate.
>
> In ozone you can pick players off and balk. Minor A players have to throw it to the plate every time they get on the mound.
>
> Minor A players run and steal bases with a short distance. Ozone players get to run and steal farther than minor A players.
>
> Minor A players get good hits, but ozone players are strong enough to hit the ball over the fence.

Figure 4.3 Jake, Fifth Grade

> Jake
>
> My Dead Dog
>
> So today when I got picked up from school my mom had told me my Dog had just died. So she told me that in a week we would get a new one. When we got to the Dog Home I ran to the first dog. It was Brown unlike my old one but lazy like mine. So I decided to Look at some others. The second one was Blond like mine but it was to wild. So I said no. The third one was blonde like mine, wasent lazy but it was a baby. So I said I liked it out on the car ride home it barfed on me Just like my old one.

Additional Texts: Compare and Contrast

Hammerhead vs. Bull Shark by Jerry Pallotta: This book (one of several in a series) features two animals and compares and contrasts their behavior and physical characteristics.

The Other Side by Jacqueline Woodson: The story compares and contrasts life for two young girls (one black and one white) living side by side, separated by a fence in a segregated community.

Stellaluna by Janell Cannon: In this fiction picture book, Stellaluna, a baby bat, falls into a nest of baby birds. The text reveals the differences between the behaviors and needs of baby birds and baby bats.

Take the Lead, George Washington, and *Stand Tall, Abe Lincoln* by Judith St. George: Use these two biographies and create a T-chart or Venn diagram to compare and contrast the lives of these two U.S. presidents.

What Do You Do with a Tail Like This? by Steve Jenkins: Many animals are shown in the story with their body parts (tails, noses, ears, eyes, feet, mouth) and the very different ways each uses its parts.

5

CAUSE AND EFFECT

It isn't difficult to imagine a young child running carelessly through the yard after a long soaking rain. Soon his shoes are drenched and covered in mud. When he needs a drink or a bathroom break, he dashes in the house and back out. Later he is completely baffled when you ask him about the trail of debris he left behind. Sometimes it seems that childhood is immune to awareness of cause and effect.

It has been our experience that cause and effect is a more challenging text structure for young readers and writers to grasp. So we suggest opening the exploration of this structure with a look at examples of cause and effect in the lives of children. Examples include:

- Flipping a light switch makes the light come on.
- Turning the handle on the faucet makes the water flow.
- Leaving the cap off a marker makes the ink dry up.
- Standing in the rain gets you wet.
- Eating too much ice cream makes your tummy hurt.
- Getting too little sleep makes you tired.
- Drinking a lot of water makes you need to go to the bathroom.
- Heavy rain causes flooding.
- Lightning causes forest fires.

- Big storms cause power outages.
- Lack of water causes a plant to die.

Establishing the concept that one event is the cause of another is necessary groundwork for understanding this text structure in both reading and writing.

Examples of cause and effect can be found in all types of writing. When texts or sections of a text are organized using cause and effect, the purpose is to explain what happened and why it happened. To identify cause and effect when reading it is helpful to look for the relationship between one event and another. As a reader you may pause and ask yourself, "What is happening here? Why is that happening?" Or you may think of it this way, "Something happened . . . because . . ." As a writer you may pause and ask yourself, "What would happen if . . . ?"

⊟ LESSON FOCUS Introduce Cause and Effect as a Text Structure

Readers, we have explored several ways writers can organize texts to help us understand when we read. Today we are going to explore cause and effect as a way to organize writing. When writers use cause and effect to organize their work for readers, they show us how one thing causes other things to happen.

We know a book where the writer uses cause and effect on almost every page. I'm sure you remember, *If You Give a Mouse a Cookie* by Laura Joffe Numeroff. I'm going to read a few pages and pause for us to talk about how one thing causes another in this story.

[Read the first few pages. Stop on the page where the mouse will ask for a napkin.]

Readers, it seems that each time the boy does something for the mouse, it causes the mouse to need one more thing. When the writer is using cause/effect to organize the text for us we can ask these two questions:

1. What happened here? (effect)

2. Why did it happen? (cause)

We could also say it this way: "Something happened . . . because . . ."

Let's try that with what we have read so far. Think for a few seconds about each thing that happened and why each thing happened.

[Pause briefly.]

Readers, share your thoughts with your partner.

[Pause briefly.]

Readers, let's make a list on the chart of what we notice [see Figure 5.1].

[Turn to the chart and draw a line down the middle. On the left note what happened here (effect). On the right, note why it happened (cause).]

I'll start and then ask you to share your thoughts.

I noticed that the boy gave the mouse a glass of milk. I asked myself, "Why did that happen?" And, of course, it's because the cookie made him thirsty.

[Write on the chart: The boy gave the mouse a glass of milk. The cookie made the mouse thirsty.]

What can you and your partner add to our list?

[Make notes as students offer comments. Scaffold as necessary to draw the connections between the cause and the effect.]

Someone said, "The boy got the mouse a straw." I'll add that on the "Something happened" side of the chart. Now tell me why he got a straw, and I'll add that on the "Because" side. [See Figure 5.1.]

I heard someone say, "The mouse got a straw because he was too little to hold the glass."

[Continue with this pattern, reading a few pages and pausing to notice and record the cause/effect connections, until you've reached the end of the book.]

If You Give A Mouse A Cookie	
Something happened...	Because...
· the boy gave the mouse a glass of milk	· the cookie made the mouse get thirsty
· the boy got a straw for the mouse	· the mouse was too little to hold the glass
· the boy gave the mouse a napkin	· the mouse got milk on his face
· the boy gave the mouse a mirror	· the mouse worried that he might have a milk moustache
· the boy gave the mouse little scissors	· the mouse noticed his hair needed a trim

Figure 5.1 If You Give a Mouse a Cookie Chart

Readers, we have done a lot of thinking today. Look at our chart full of cause/effect connections. As you move back to your reading spot to begin independent reading you may notice the writer is using a cause/effect connection in what you are reading. If you do, place a sticky note on the page, and let's explore how it helps you make meaning as you read.

R eaders, we are going to continue our exploration of cause and effect. Remember, if the writer is using cause and effect, it can be helpful to ask, "What happened here?" and "Why did that happen?" or "Something happened . . . because . . ."

Yesterday we read *Chrysanthemum* by Kevin Henkes for our read-aloud story. Let's return to the pages near the beginning of the story. Remember in the beginning Chrysanthemum loves her name. Let's read those pages again with careful attention to the language and the art.

[Read the first five pages of the story.]

So we have seen pictures of Chrysanthemum smiling and looking happy. We saw one speech bubble where she says, "I love my name!" The narrator tells us she loves the way her name sounds, and she loves the way it looks. It's pretty clear that Chrysanthemum *loves* her name right now. Let's make a chart to help us see what is going on with Chrysanthemum. [See Figure 5.2a.]

But when she begins school . . . something happens . . . because . . .

Readers, as I read the next few pages, remember to listen closely to the language and to look closely at the illustrations. After a few pages I will ask you to think about something that happened . . . because . . .

[Read the next five pages of the story.]

Readers, something changed. Think about what just happened and why it happened. Remember it may help to say it this way: Something happened . . . because . . .

[Pause for reflection.]

So, something happened. Talk with your partner about what changed in this part. Decide why that happened. Something happened . . . because . . .

[Pause briefly for partners to name the change and the reasons.]

OK, let's get some of your thoughts on our chart. I'll write what happened in the left column. Then, we will think about why it happened and write that on the right. I'm ready; let me hear from a few of you.

Several of you are saying the big change is that Chrysanthemum does not like her name now. That would be the "something happened" part. Now let's list the "because" part. I'll add that on the right. [See Figure 5.2b.]

[Summarize the chart by reminding students how the author used cause and effect to help us make sense. As you reach the end of the list, bring closure to the lesson by summarizing the cause/effects connections. Continue the exploration of cause and effect with other texts.]

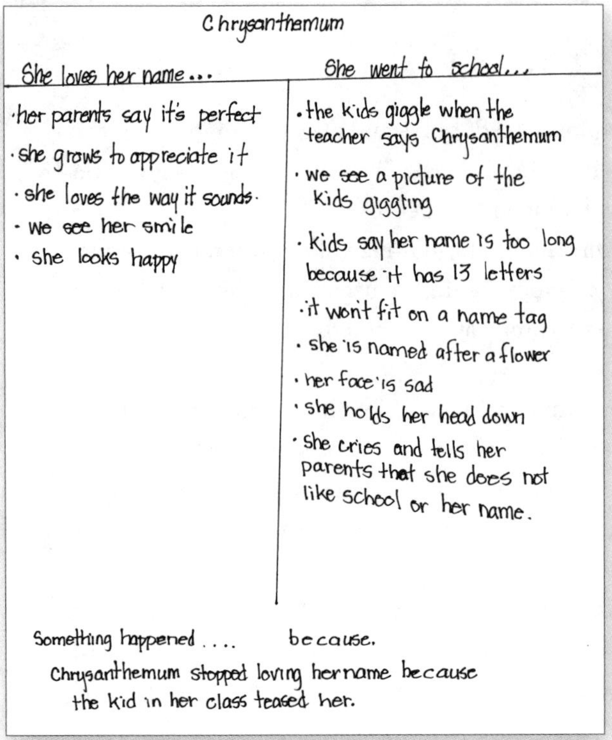

Figure 5.2a Chrysanthemum Chart

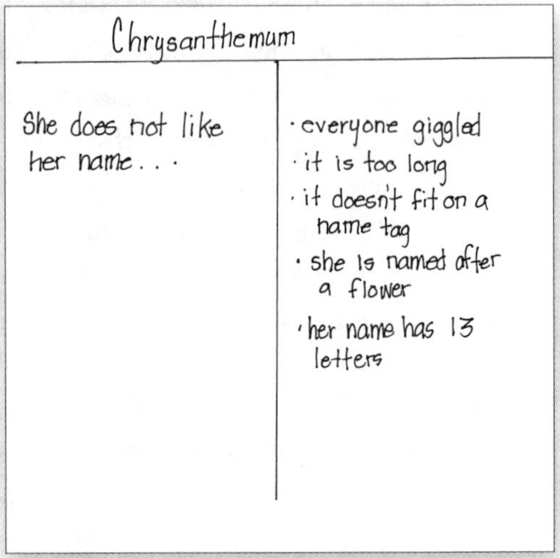

Figure 5.2b Chrysanthemum Chart

Flip It from Reading to Writing

Gaining insight into the relationship between cause and effect enables the reader to predict outcomes and understand the impact of a decision within the text upon the outcomes revealed at the conclusion. When that insight is flipped the writer is positioned to foreshadow events, to allude to an outcome, and to bridge the space between two events linking the cause with the outcome or effect. The writer must recognize the relationship between the cause and effect and must understand both when and how to execute the structure effectively.

Writers, we have explored many ways of organizing our work. And the last text structure we worked with in reading was cause and effect. You'll remember *If You Give a Mouse a Cookie* by Laura Joffe Numeroff and *Chrysanthemum* by Kevin Henkes were two of the books we explored while learning how a writer can use cause and effect to help us make sense when we read. Today we are going to flip our learning over from reading to writing. Let's explore how to organize our texts with cause and effect to help our readers make sense of our writing. We can start with a review of what we learned from those two books.

[Review the charts with attention to the questions: What happened? Why did that happen? Or Something happened . . . because . . .]

Writers, we can use cause and effect in our work when we want the reader to know how one thing caused another thing to happen.

Last night I was reading through my notebook thinking about how one thing often causes another. I remembered a day last summer when I was stung by three bees. I know it was my fault because I got scared and tried to swat the bees away with my book.

Writers, first I thought about what happened, and I made a list. I'll share it with you. [Turn your notebook so students can see the list. Read your list aloud.]

- I was reading outside by the flowers.
- Bees were buzzing around.
- A bee got too close to me.
- I was frightened.
- I swatted at the bee with my book.
- I got stung.
- My arm hurt.
- I cried.
- My arm swelled up, and big red welts came up on it.
- My neighbor took me to the emergency room.
- The doctor told me I am allergic to bee stings.
- I got a shot that helped.

As I reread my list I noticed that each one of these things was a cause/effect connection, just like in the book *If You Give a Mouse a Cookie*. I decided cause and effect would be a good way to organize this narrative.

I was thinking about *If You Give a Mouse a Cookie* and tried to remember how each thing in that story leads to the next thing. Here's what I wrote:

> *Last summer I was reading outside by the flowers. Bees were flying all around the blossoms. I could hear the buzzing as they zipped by. When one bee got too close, I got frightened and waved my book hoping it would fly away. The next thing I knew I was getting stung by bees. I ran into the house trying to get away from them. I was crying because my arm was hurting so much. I put ice on the stings, but my arm began to swell. I had a big red welt rising up around the sting. Even my tongue began to swell, and it was difficult to talk. Thank goodness my neighbor was home to take me to the emergency room. The doctor said I was allergic to bee stings and gave me a shot that helped a lot.*

Let's check my narrative to see if I have used cause and effect to keep it organized. Remember we can check our writing using the questions a reader would ask: 1) What things happened? 2) Why did those things happen? Or Something happened . . . because . . . . Let's go through my narrative and make a list of what happened and why.

[Make a list on the chart as the students recall the events. Scaffold as needed to support the connections between cause and effect. Your chart may include connections like these:

- Bees were buzzing around the flowers because they wanted to get nectar.
- I got scared because the bees got too close.
- The bees got defensive because I waved the book at them.
- The bees stung me because I was a threat to them when I was waving my book around.
- My arm began to hurt because the bees stung me.
- I cried because the bee stings hurt a lot.
- My arm and tongue began to swell because I'm allergic to bee stings.
- It was difficult for me to talk because my tongue was swelling.
- My neighbor drove me to the emergency room because I was really scared.

❖ The doctor gave me a shot because she could tell I was allergic to bee stings.]

Writers, let's have a go at using cause and effect in a narrative. You may begin searching your notebook or thinking about an event where something happened to you. Remember we are using cause and effect to help us organize, so you will need to think about the two questions a reader would ask: 1) What happened? 2) Why did it happen? or Something happened . . . because . . . .

If you are thinking of something new, be sure to jot it in your notebook.

[Allow time for thinking and topic exploration.]

Writers, zoom in on one idea you think will work best and share that one with your partner.

[Allow time for sharing.]

Thumbs up if you have an idea ready to go.

[Note whether there are students who seem unsure.]

When you get to your writing spot you may choose to begin by making a list the way I did in my notebook. Then think about what happened and why it happened as you begin to write.

Off we go, it's time to write.

Writing Samples

Avery uses a cause/effect structure in this text to reveal the dangers of jumping on a trampoline with a ball (see Figure 5.3).

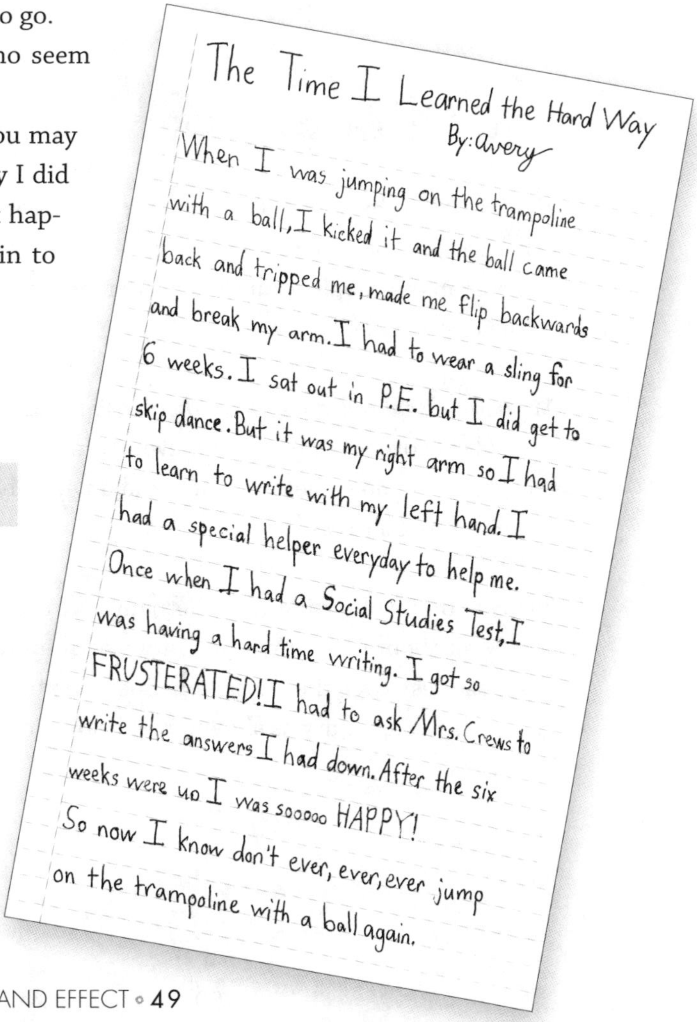

Figure 5.3 Avery, Fourth Grade

> The Time I Learned the Hard Way
> By: Avery
>
> When I was jumping on the trampoline with a ball, I kicked it and the ball came back and tripped me, made me flip backwards and break my arm. I had to wear a sling for 6 weeks. I sat out in P.E. but I did get to skip dance. But it was my right arm so I had to learn to write with my left hand. I had a special helper everyday to help me. Once when I had a Social Studies Test, I was having a hard time writing. I got so FRUSTERATED! I had to ask Mrs. Crews to write the answers I had down. After the six weeks were up I was soooo HAPPY! So now I know don't ever, ever, ever jump on the trampoline with a ball again.

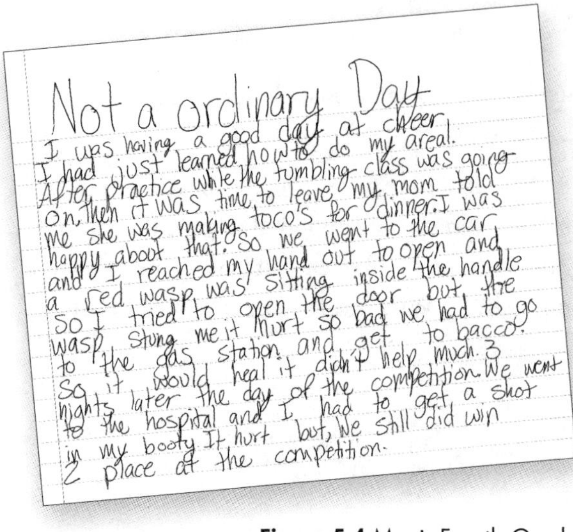
Not a ordinary Day
I was having a good day at cheer.
I had just learned how to do my areal.
After practice while the tumbling class was going
on. Then it was time to leave, my mom told
me she was making toco's for dinner. I was
happy about that. So we went to the car
and I reached my hand out to open and
a red wasp was sitting inside the handle
So I tried to open the door but the
wasp stung me it hurt so bad we had to go
to the gas station and get to bacco.
So it would heal it didn't help much. 3
nights later the day of the competition. We went
to the hospital and I had to get a shot
in my booty It hurt but, we still did win
2 place at the competition.

Figure 5.4 Maci, Fourth Grade

Maci talks about an ordinary day with an unexpected event that put a kink in her day. The cause/effect structure helps her bring focus to that event (see Figure 5.4).

Additional Texts: Cause and Effect

The Lotus Seed by Sherry Garland: The cause for the turmoil in the story was the rule of other nations over Vietnam, leaving people with little choice of how they lived. The effect was that many people escaped the country, leaving their treasures behind never to return to their homeland.

My Rotten Redheaded Older Brother by Patricia Polacco: Polacco played "second fiddle" to her older brother who could do everything well. Because of this sibling rivalry, Polacco tried hard to find something she could do equally as well. But regardless of what she tried she never met success.

The Wall by Eve Bunting: The Vietnam War caused many things as described in this picture book about the war monument in Washington, DC. Effects include the death of loved ones, sadness over their loss, loneliness from seeing their names inscribed on the wall, and devastating injury as shown by the soldier visiting the monument to salute his fallen comrades.

WEAVING MEANING

The human mind seeks meaning. We strive to make sense out of what is happening to us and around us. We seek order in chaos, we look for patterns and connections that will help us put ideas and experiences into some perspective, and we strive to find some relevance. When ideas, thoughts, and experiences fail to make sense, we struggle to find meaning there, or we eventually let them go.

Comprehension is meaning making. It is the fabric made of threads pulled from what is known, believed, understood, felt, and experienced, all woven together with threads from the language, thoughts, images, and ideas presented in the text. It is not what lies dormant on the page. Nor is it what we hold in our minds. We believe that meaning is more than the writer's intentions. It is more than the reader's ability to vocalize the words of the text. Meaning is more than the contribution of either the writer or the reader. Meaning materializes when these threads are woven together to create something more than either held alone. Meaning is the fabric we weave out of our engagement with texts. As such the meaning made by each reader will have threads in common with many other readers and threads that are specific to the individual reader.

In this section we will examine what have come to be known as standard aspects of comprehension. Though we realize there are many, we have selected a few to demonstrate the reciprocal relationship between reading and writing. We take those one at a time to look closely and draw the connections between what is required of the reader and what is required of the writer.

Making meaning is an integrated act, for both reader and writer, weaving all the individual threads into an integrated whole in the process of making meaning. Clearly, there are times when one thread is prominent and others are more subdued, but the fabric of meaning is made up of all the threads.

Background Knowledge

Generally, background knowledge is defined as the total of all information and experience a learner brings to any task. Background knowledge, then, is a critical factor in students' ability to make meaning from the texts they encounter. It is our contention that background knowledge is the stockroom of fibers from which readers and writers select as they weave meaning using any strategy we teach them.

It is easy to see the importance of background knowledge when watching young children approach a new learning task. Successful students begin to tap into their background knowledge by asking questions and wondering how the new fits with what they already know. They begin to weave their known and the new into some interpretation. Students with a less well-developed store of background knowledge struggle to weave new insights and generate less insightful questions.

Several years ago while working as an elementary principal, Reba had an experience that revealed the importance of assessing the background knowledge of students in new situations. A third grader—we will call him John—was sent to the office following his disruptive behavior during the showing of a video on Rosa Parks.

In a conversation with John it became very clear that his background knowledge of the civil rights movement was very limited, and he knew nothing about Rosa Parks or her role in the movement. As the conversation moved along Reba pulled a few picture books from her shelf and read with John to help him build a bit of background and a sense of the history of Mrs. Parks' remarkable act of courage. As Reba and John read together and talked about the books, she noticed a visible shift in his posture and attitude; he began to show interest and appreciation. John may have entered the office filled with frustration and resentment, but he left more informed and bubbling with questions and new interest in the civil rights movement, especially with the role of Rosa Parks.

In that short visit with his principal, John had been given the opportunity to add information, gain insight, layer in new vocabulary, and build interest that he could weave into his viewing of the video and the reading that would follow. That small start equipped John to ask questions and add more information, not only about Rosa Parks but also about the civil rights movement in general.

The lack of background knowledge doesn't always result in frustration and acting out. In fact, we may well engage in the process of building background knowledge when 1) we recognize the gap ourselves and 2) understand that developing background serves a real function for us.

A few significant things to remember:

◆ We need to help our students recognize when their knowledge is limited and help them develop strategies to independently build that background.

◆ Learners are willing to pursue background when they have purpose for that information. It must matter to them. We tend to forget that our giving an assignment is not the same as purpose-driven engagement.

◆ Learners must trust there are accessible resources. Our students have to trust that there is no penalty for not knowing. They must feel safe to risk revealing they don't know. We must develop a culture that celebrates the desire to know.

Activate and expand background knowledge via

◆ read-alouds

◆ writing as reflection on reading

◆ field trips/direct experiences

◆ videos/digital media/vicarious experiences

◆ journal writing/writer's notebook/quick writes

- interviews/dialog/conversation
- research
- independent reading

Our favorite way to activate and expand students' background knowledge is to read aloud. We carefully select picture books and sequence them so that each book scaffolds for the next. Each book then layers in vocabulary, helps develop a contextual framework, and begins to create a bank of images (Laminack and Wadsworth 2006a; Laminack and Wadsworth 2006b; Laminack 2009). This series of read-aloud experiences paired with dialog is followed with a small collection of texts made available for independent reading throughout the unit of study.

Flip It: Background Knowledge

Background knowledge is equally important to writers. Writers need background information to generate text just as readers need background knowledge to weave meaning from their interaction with a text. Writers pull from their experiences, memories, passions, and interests. There are times when writers generate new texts without pulling a single reference because they are writing from what is already known to them. Then, there are times when writers become interested in a topic about which they have limited knowledge. Their interest in the topic sparks a search for more information and deeper insight. That search may lead them to explore the topic through reading, travel, interviews, music, videos, web searches, and other types of research needed to build background substantial enough to support the writing they have planned.

Lester is working on a picture book manuscript, and the main character lives with a beekeeper. The idea for the story was sparked by a life event told to him a couple of years ago. The event gave Lester the seed for the plot, but his knowledge of honeybees and beekeeping was rather sparse. So he made notes for the story idea and then set out in search of information because he knew, even with fiction, the information layered in about bees has to be believable and accurate.

Not unlike your students, Lester went online where he found countless sites and was quickly overwhelmed by the depth of information there. So he decided to begin with much more basic information and pulled nonfiction picture books on honeybees from his library. He read each book and made notes and generated questions that led him back to a web search for more specific information. The visit to basic, simple information helped him discover enough to ask more focused questions and further his understanding. That information was necessary to weave a believable story.

Like Lester our students are reader-writers (readers *and* writers simultaneously). Background knowledge is a resource in service to them at all times. Writers draw upon background knowledge, searching for relevant threads to weave a text they will present to their readers. Readers draw upon background knowledge, searching for relevant threads to weave into what writers presented.

Background knowledge is a supply room of sorts, the place we turn to when we need relevant threads to weave meaning. Those threads hold potential, yet are not sufficient. The weaver must have skill to select the threads, create the design, and weave them together into a coherent whole. And so it is with reader-writers. The skills and strategies we employ as readers are employed in the daily thinking of children. We seek to help children see the intersection of their thinking, their reading, and their writing.

Background knowledge is an essential factor in the weaving of meaning. It is tapped by every comprehension strategy we teach readers. In this section we will explore a set of comprehension strategies commonly included in reading instruction and examine how reader insights for each can become opportunities for writing growth.

6

INFERRING

An inference is a natural thing. A child looks out the window upon waking and notices there are puddles on the sidewalks and droplets balanced on blades of grass. The child says, "It rained last night. I didn't even hear it."

That's an inference.

No one announced that it rained during the night while everyone slept. The child saw evidence outside her window and wove that information into the threads of her experiences and prior knowledge to arrive at an inference.

Though it may be natural to infer, not all inferences lead to fact or truth. Suppose the puddles and droplets were the result of a sprinkler system. To connect what is presented with what is known results in a possibility, which may not be accurate. Now, if our young girl were to walk out to the edge of the drive and pick up the morning paper, she would notice that the street is dry. That new information would be added to the fabric and result in a new inference. "Ah, it didn't rain. It was only the sprinkler." An inference is a conclusion reached when we close the gap between what is *presented to us* and what is *present within us*.

Even toddlers make inferences of a sort. Many of you have witnessed the excitement that ensues when an adult opens the closet and takes out a coat and picks up the keys and the car seat. The toddler reacts, inferring that a car trip is soon to follow. That assumption arises from patterns of behavior that have built an experiential memory, background knowledge, and a schema for car trips.

"Inference is part rational, part mystical, part definable, and part beyond definition. Individuals' life experiences, logic, wisdom, values, creativity, and thoughtfulness, set against the text they are reading, form the crux of new meaning. Because each person's experiences are different, the art of inferring takes the reader beyond the text to a place only he or she can go. When we read, we can choose to limit our interpretations to the literal words of the text, but by doing so we greatly limit understanding" (Keene and Zimmermann 2007, 145).

Imagine a writer as one who assembles a jigsaw puzzle. He has the advantage of viewing the image on the box lid to guide him. Let's say the image is a farm. He closely studies the image and sorts the pieces into small piles. The red pieces will be the barn. The browns will be the two horses grazing in the pasture. The green pieces will form the grassy areas. The scattered blues and whites will be the cloudy sky. Soon he begins to assemble. Perhaps he works the edges first and builds a frame, or perhaps he zooms in on the red barn, working with the small pile of pieces to assemble that image first. As the puzzle comes together, the writer can selectively leave pieces out, giving the viewer an opportunity to participate in constructing the image.

The writer knows that a reader is more likely to engage when her brain has to become actively involved and is therefore deliberate in his choice of what to leave out. There must be enough context for the reader to make the connection between what is present and what is missing. And the writer must be conscious of the reader to assume she has some schema for the image he is laying out. There comes a time when the writer has assembled the puzzle and he leaves it for others to read . . . to see the image, to feel, to experience, to make meaning.

The reader views this puzzle. She finds the assembled pieces create an image. And though the writer left out a few pieces here and there, the reader is able to fill in what is missing. She is able to assemble the image in her mind. The writer was working from a plan, a vision of what he hoped to achieve. That vision was his guide as he assembled the puzzle. The reader didn't share that plan. However, she has a schema for rural life. She has prior knowledge of farms and is able to recognize the pastoral scene of rolling hills, a cloud-spotted sky, the weathered red barn, and the peaceful horses grazing in green pastures. She recognizes the subject as rural farm life. She knows the relationship between horses and grass and barns. She knows enough to imagine how the hills roll on beyond the borders of what is present. She knows enough to focus on the image and hear the wind blow. She can smell the old wood and the hay and the manure and the sweat of horses in the barn. She can hear the horses whinny and snort and stomp. She can hear the old barn creak in the wind. She can weave the fabric of personal understanding from the fibers given her by the writer and those she brings from her own experience and knowledge. She closes the gap between what is presented and what is present within her. In short, she infers.

Because the writer and the reader share that much, they are able to build meaning together, even if they never meet in person. They weave the given and the shared into a fabric of understanding.

Inferences do not happen out of thin air. In order for a reader to infer, a writer has to set the stage. Inferring, though done in the mind of the reader, is frontloaded by a writer. The writer implies and alludes. The writer shows emotion through a character's actions and reactions. The writer gives us glimpses of thought and motive and actions and attitudes through conversations with the character and about the character. If the writer assumes too much, the reader may not share enough to weave her known into what is given by the writer. Writers set the stage for readers in a number of ways. Keene and Zimmermann (2007) remind us that "[i]t may be true that the reader has more latitude to infer in fiction, memoir, and poetry, but we must infer when reading nonfiction text as well. To push beyond a dry, literal understanding, to add our own opinions, knowledge, and ideas—*that is to infer*" (146).

⊷ LESSON FOCUS Introduce the Concept of Inferring

Readers, if we were walking down the hallway and saw a mop and bucket just outside the door to the library, what would you think had happened?

Don't say anything yet. Let's pause to sit with this image in our minds. Close your eyes and think about seeing that mop and bucket just outside the library door. Think about why it's there. Think about what seeing that tells you.

[Pause briefly.]

Readers, share your thoughts with your partner. Be sure you listen as well. Let's see what ideas this sparks in our minds.

[Pause briefly as students share.]

I'd like to hear from a few of you. Someone share what your partner had to say about that mop and bucket outside the library door. I'll jot your comments in my notebook. OK, I'm ready.

[Allow a few students to share their thoughts.]

So far this is what I've jotted:

- ◆ Someone got sick and the custodian came to clean it up.

- ◆ Someone spilled something in the library and went to get the mop to clean up.

- The custodian mopped the library while no one was in there.
- The custodian was on his way to mop the floor somewhere and stopped to get a book.

We are thinking like readers today. We had just a bit of information, and we tapped into what we already know to figure out what might be happening in the library. Let's consider these ideas and think about how we came up with each of them.

Someone got sick and the custodian had to come clean it up. We know that sometimes a kid does get sick at school, and when that happens we typically call the custodian to bring the mop.

Someone spilled something in the library and went to get the mop to clean up. We know there are times when things get spilled. When that happens we call the custodian or borrow the mop and clean up.

The custodian mopped the library while no one was in there. We know that the custodian mops all the floors in our school. And we know he can't mop them while we are in the room working.

The custodian was on his way to mop the floor somewhere and he stopped to get a book. We know that the custodian is a busy man. He is always cleaning someplace in the school. But we also know he likes to read. We have seen him reading in the lunchroom. He has come to read to us. We have seen his favorite books posted on the wall by his supply closet.

Readers, there are times when the writer gives us a few details and expects us to fill in a few more details from our brains. Today all we knew was that the mop and bucket had been left in the hall next to the library door. But we didn't know for sure why, so we used our brains to think about what could be happening. That is called inferring.

We had to infer the story to explain why the mop and bucket were in the hall.

Sometimes, as readers, we infer something and read on to find out that we got the wrong idea. Then we reread and correct our thinking.

When we were thinking about why the mop and bucket had been left by the library door, we didn't start with wild guesses. We stopped to think about what we know. Remember how we took about forty seconds to sit and think? We closed our eyes and thought about seeing that mop and bucket sitting in the hallway.

Inferring is not just guessing. Inferring is using what we know and what the writer gives us and weaving them together to make sense of what we are reading. Today each of you took what you know about school and our custodian and what you know about the mop and bucket, and you used all of that to infer what was happening. Everything you said makes sense. Every idea is something that has happened at school; it is something that could really happen. So each of those ideas makes sense. But, the only way we can be certain is to get more information. When we are reading we need to read on, to get more information and see what makes sense. If we want to find out for sure why the mop and bucket were left next to the library door we need to get more information, so we would go ask the custodian.

Readers, our brains infer all the time because inferring is a very important way to make meaning. Over the next several days we will be exploring texts where the writer expects us to infer as we read. We will examine those places in each text carefully and pay close attention to our thinking and consider what the writer did to set us up.

◼ LESSON FOCUS Exploring Opportunities to Infer as Readers

Readers, yesterday we talked about inferring and the way our brains are always working to make meaning when we read. Today we are going to revisit one of our best friend books, *Jamaica's Find* by Juanita Havill. You know this story very well, but I'm going to read it aloud to you. I'll stop in a few spots where Juanita expects us to infer. There are places where Juanita tells us what Jamaica says, but our brains have to fill in the rest and infer what Jamaica was feeling and thinking.

[Hold up the book so the cover is visible for everyone. Open to the first spread and read. Pause on the spread where Jamaica arrives home with the stuffed dog.]

Readers, I'm pausing here for a moment because we have to infer something on this page. Juanita tells us what Jamaica and her mom said to each other. But she doesn't tell us what Jamaica did or what she was thinking. We have to infer that part.

When mom says she is glad that Jamaica returned the hat, Jamaica says the hat didn't fit her. We can infer something Jamaica did. Let's pause and let our brains work. What does this tell us that Jamaica did with that hat before she turned it in?

[Pause briefly as they consider this.]

Readers, I'll tell you what I inferred here. I'm thinking Jamaica tried on that hat because she was thinking about bringing it home with the dog. I'm thinking she turned it in at Lost and Found only because it didn't fit her.

Give me a thumbs up if you agree.

Let's return to this page [Hold the book up open to the page you just read.] and read it one more time. This time I'd like you to think about what Juanita Havill did to help us infer.

[Read the page again. Don't rush.]

Readers, let's begin thinking about how we know what Jamaica did.

1. We didn't see Jamaica try on the hat in the illustration.

2. Juanita didn't tell us that Jamaica tried on the hat.

3. But we *know* that she did try on the hat because Juanita Havill *did* tell us that Jamaica said, "It didn't fit me."

4. Our brains know that Jamaica would have to try on that hat to find out if it fit.

So one way an author can help us infer is to use dialog where the character talks about what she did.

I'm going to read a few more pages. I'll pause again when there is something for us to infer. But this time when I stop I'll ask you to do the thinking.

[Hold the book out facing the students, and read aloud the next four spreads, stopping after you read the page where Jamaica and her mom are sitting on the bed together.]

Readers, now we know more about what everyone *said* and *did*. This time we have to infer what Jamaica was *feeling* in this scene. Take a moment to think about what Jamaica is *feeling* when she is sitting in her room.

[Pause briefly and allow them time to sit with this idea.]

Readers, share your thoughts with your partner.

[Again, pause very briefly as they exchange thoughts.]

Let's hear from a few of you.

[Allow time for a few students to share what they and their partners were thinking.]

Readers, it seems we are inferring that Jamaica is feeling sad and perhaps a bit guilty. I heard someone say Jamaica feels embarrassed. And someone inferred that Jamaica feels that she should have turned in the dog when she turned in the hat. So maybe she is feeling *remorseful*. I think we can agree we are inferring that Jamaica feels she did not make the best choice and she wants to fix it.

How did Juanita Havill help us make this inference? Let's look back at those pages and see what Juanita *does* give us and how that helps our brains infer.

Let's take a look

[Turn back to the page where the family is gathering at the table.]

On these pages we hear her family saying the dog isn't very clean and she can't have it in the kitchen. Juanita tells us that Jamaica hears her mother say the dog probably belongs to another little girl.

[Turn the page.]

And on these pages Juanita tells us that Jamaica looked closely at the dog and then tossed it on a chair.

That's when my brain began to infer that Jamaica was feeling bad about her decision.

So another way a writer can help us to infer is by showing us what the character does and how the character changes.

Readers, there are two more places where we will stop to infer. As I read this time, notice how your brain will already be filling in parts and making meaning.

[Turn the page. Read only the one page.]

Hmmm, what are you inferring here? Turn to your partner and share your thoughts.

[Pause briefly while they share ideas.]

Let me hear your thoughts.

[Listen as a few students share their thoughts, then summarize for the group.]

Readers, some of us were inferring how Jamaica feels when she turned in the dog. We said she is embarrassed and maybe feeling guilty. Some of us were inferring what Jamaica was thinking. We said she is thinking that the man knows she took the dog yesterday. And we said she is hoping that the man will tell her she can keep the dog.

Our brains are doing a lot of work on this one page.

I'll read this page again. This time notice what Juanita does to help us infer what Jamaica was thinking and feeling.

[Reread the page.]

Readers, what did you notice?

[Pause briefly to allow a few students to comment, then summarize for the group.]

Juanita told us that Jamaica felt hot around her ears. And our brains know that means she may be feeling embarrassed or guilty. Juanita told us how Jamaica's ears felt. We had to infer what that tells us about how that made her feel in her heart.

So another way a writer can help us to infer is to give us details about the character's reaction to a situation.

Remember that some of us inferred that Jamaica was hoping the man would tell her to keep the dog. Can you talk about what Juanita did that helped you infer that?

[Pause briefly for a few comments.]

Juanita lets us see Jamaica waiting there. And she lets us hear the man ask her if she found anything else. Then Jamaica still waits at the counter to watch the man put the dog on the shelf until he tells her some kid will come get it soon. Watching Jamaica linger helps our brains infer that she still really wants to keep the dog.

So now we see a writer shows what the character does to help us infer what the character is thinking.

We are doing a lot of inferring in this story. I'll read the last few pages.

[Read to the end of the book.]

It's good to revisit a best friend book. I'm always surprised how much we can discover each time we do. Readers, today as you are back in your spot reading this morning, I'd like you to notice when your brain is making an inference and think about what the writer does to help.

Flip It from Reading to Writing

Remember that readers infer as they make meaning. Readers need to infer when writers imply, suggest, allude to, describe, have characters share emotions, use metaphor/simile or poetic language, and reveal part of the meaning.

◄ LESSON FOCUS Exploring Opportunities to Infer as Writers

Writers, we have been exploring strategies to help us make meaning when we read. When we read *Jamaica's Find* by Juanita Havill, there were a few places where we had to infer what Jamaica was thinking or feeling. The writer, Juanita Havill, told us a lot of what Jamaica said, and she described much of what Jamaica did. But we had to infer what Jamaica was thinking and how she was feeling.

That got me thinking about the writing we have been doing recently. Sometimes I tell the reader everything, and then she doesn't have to infer. Today I'm going to take something from my notebook and ask you to help me revise it. I want to revise what I have so the reader will need to get involved and think about what is happening. I'd like you to help me rewrite a segment.

I'll show you what I have now. [See Figure 6.1.]

[Show the page in your notebook. If possible project the image with a document camera or have a copy of the page for each pair of partners.]

I'll read this aloud for us.

[Read the segment aloud.]

Writers, notice that I'm telling you about how Sam feels here. I need your help with two spots in this scene. The first one is when Sam is coming into school. I *tell* you that he feels really happy. The second one is when Nathan says unkind things to him. I *tell* you that Sam feels awful.

I would like to revise this scene so my readers have to get involved and infer how Sam feels. I want to use other details the way that Juanita Havill did in *Jamaica's Find*.

Work with your partner, and think of a few ways I might revise this to help my readers infer.

[Pause to allow time for the partners to reread and generate alternatives.]

Writers, I'm hearing several options as you work together. Let's pause a moment to share what you have come up with. I'll write them in my notebook so I can think about them for a while before I revise.

[Pause briefly, allowing a few students to offer options.]

Writers, here are the suggestions I wrote as you were sharing.

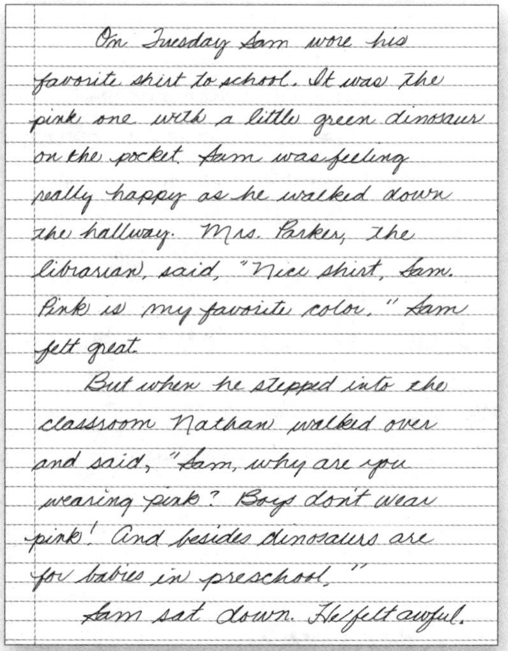

Figure 6.1 Notebook Page

Instead of saying Sam was feeling really happy

- ◆ I could describe how he moved down the hall. Maybe he hopped or skipped.

- ◆ I could write what he says. Maybe he says "Thanks, Mrs. Parker. It's my favorite color, too."

- ◆ I could describe how he stands. Sam stood a little taller and walked toward his classroom. He seemed to be walking on air.

Instead of saying Sam felt awful

- ◆ I could describe how his face changes. Sam's smile melted into a frown.

- ◆ I could describe how his posture changes. Sam slumped into his chair. Sam tried to make himself smaller. He wished he could be invisible.

Writers, thank you. I have several options to try out in my revisions. I have some thinking to do. Today as you return to your writing spot I'd like you to select a piece of your writing. Choose one you finished earlier, and read through with your partner. Look for one scene you could revise that will give your reader an opportunity to infer.

Writing Samples

Morgan uses her insights about inferring to revise her draft and set up opportunities for readers to think and engage with her text. Notice how she revises the opening lines (see Figure 6.2).

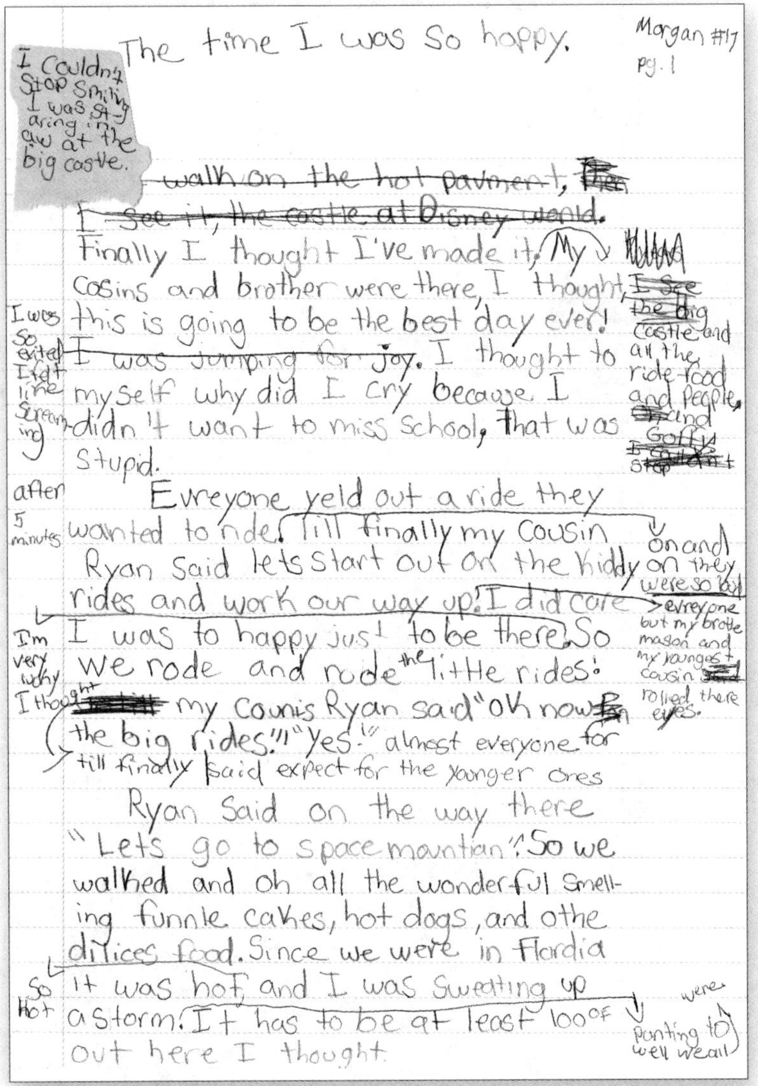

The time I was So happy.   Morgan #17
                                            pg. 1

I couldn't Stop smiling I was staring in aw at the big castle.

~~walk on the hot pavment,~~ ~~I see it, the castle at Disney world.~~
Finally I thought I've made it, My
cosins and brother were there, I thought, this is going to be the best day ever! ~~I was Jumping for joy.~~ I thought to myself why did I cry because I didn't want to miss school, that was stupid.

I was So exited I felt like Scream ing

I see the big castle and all the ride food and people, and Goffy stop it

after 5 minutes   Everyone yeld out a ride they wanted to ride, Till finally my cousin Ryan Said lets start out on the kiddy rides and work our way up! I did core I was to happy just to be there. So we rode and rode the little rides.

on and on they were so bord
everyone but my brother mason and my youngest cousin rolled there eyes.

I'm very why   I ~~thought~~ my counis Ryan said "ok now the big rides!" "Yes!" almost everyone said expect for the younger ones till finally

Ryan Said on the way there "Lets go to space mauntian". So we walked and oh all the wonderful smell-ing funnle cakes, hot dogs, and othe dilices food. Since we were in Flordia So Hot   it was hot, and I was sweating up a storm. It has to be at least 100°F out here I thought

were panting to well we all

Figure 6.2 Morgan, Fifth Grade—page 1, draft 1

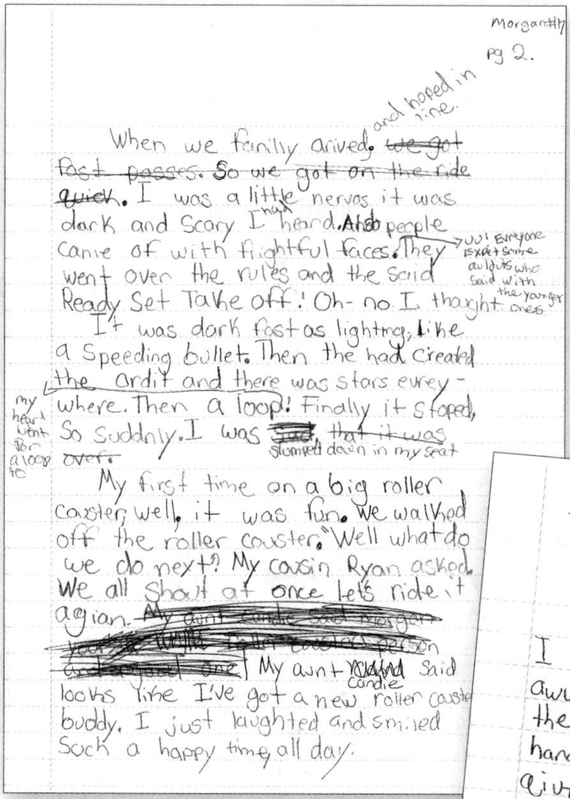

Figure 6.2 Morgan, Fifth Grade— page 2, draft 1

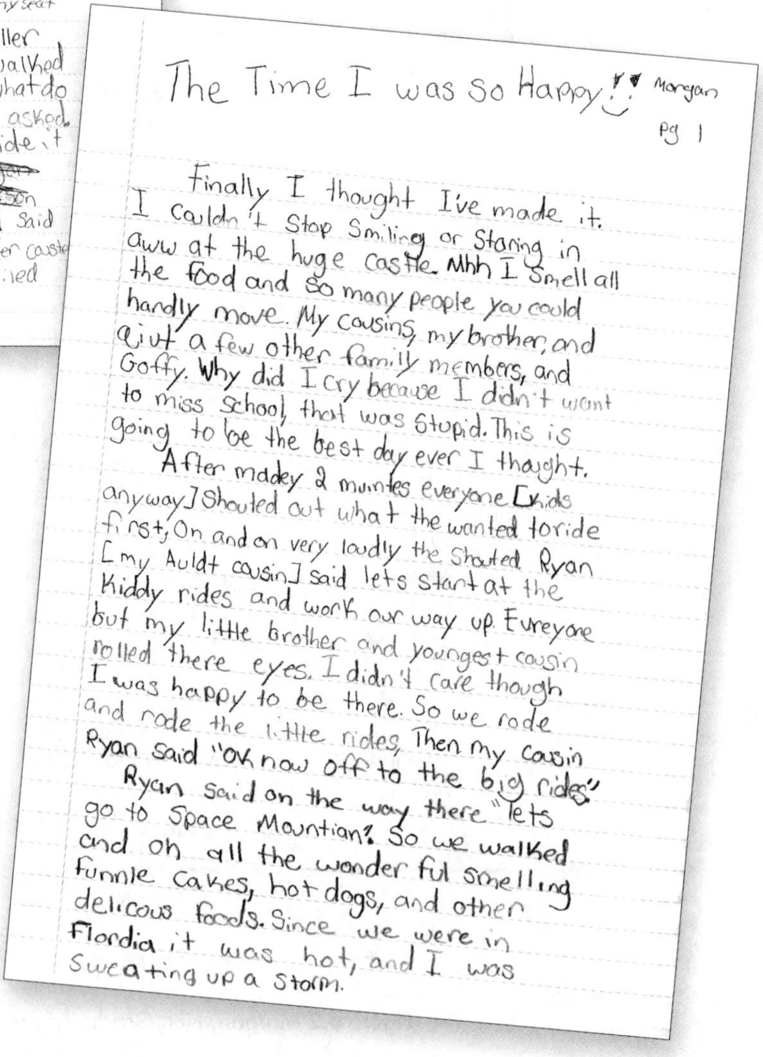

Figure 6.2 Morgan, Fifth Grade— revised paper

Morgan(?) pg 2.

When we finally arived, ~~we got fast passes~~. So we got on the ride ~~quick~~. I was a little nervos it was dark and scary I had heard. And people came of with frightful faces. They went over the rules and the said Ready Set Take off! Oh- no I thaught.

It was dark fast as lightnig, like a speeding bullet. Then the had creaded the ardit and there was stars every- where. Then a loop! Finally it stoped, So Suddnly. I was ~~that it was slumped down in my seat~~ over to.

My first time on a big roller couster well, it was fun. We walked off the roller couster. Well what do we do next? My cousin Ryan asked. We all shout at once lets ride it agian. ~~...~~ My aunt candie said looks like I've got a new roller couster buddy. I just laughted and smiled Such a happy time all day.

The Time I was So Happy!! Morgan pg 1

Finally I thought I've made it. I couldn't stop smiling or staring in aww at the huge castle. Ahh I smell all the food and so many people you could hardly move. My cousins, my brother, and aiut a few other family members, and Goffy. Why did I cry because I didn't want to miss school, that was stupid. This is going to be the best day ever I thaught.

After maddey 2 muintes everyone [kids anyway] shouted out what the wanted to ride first, On and on very loudly the shouted. Ryan [my Auldt cousin] said lets start at the kiddy rides and work our way up. Eureyone but my little brother and youngest cousin rolled there eyes. I didn't care though I was happy to be there. So we rode and rode the little rides, Then my cousin Ryan said "ok now off to the big rides"

Ryan said on the way there "lets go to Space Mountian? So we walked and oh all the wonder ful smelling funnle cakes, hot dogs, and other delicous foods. Since we were in Flordia it was hot, and I was sweating up a storm.

Additional Texts: Inferring

Gleam and Glow by Eve Bunting: As the war moves closer and closer to their home, Father feels he can no longer avoid going "underground" to fight for his country. This decision means leaving his family behind. When Mother decides the war is getting too close, she and the children flee their home. Many decisions must be made as they prepare to walk away and travel a great distance to safety. This is a complex story with many opportunities to infer about the dangers, why they leave certain things behind, and whether the father will be united with his family.

Helen's Big World: The Life of Helen Keller by Doreen Rappaport: As Helen begins to experience the loss of sight, hearing, and speech, Doreen provides opportunities for readers to infer Helen's emotions. Doreen describes other situations where Helen would get frustrated and have outbursts when others didn't understand. The text proceeds to Helen's breakthrough, understanding the association between words and objects. At each phase of Helen's life, readers infer her emotions from her actions.

Something Beautiful by Sharon Dennis Wyeth: A young girl roams her dreary neighborhood looking for something beautiful like the example given by her teacher. Each page offers an opportunity to infer what needs to be done to repair and rejuvenate the neighborhood and make it into something beautiful. As the young girl talks with her neighbors she comes to realize that beauty is seen differently by each of them.

7

SUMMARIZING

People summarize to help them hold on to the important details needed to make sense and get things done. For example, when someone is giving directions we listen carefully and note important bits such as turns and landmarks. Then, we condense that information. Perhaps we repeat it to the person who offered the directions, just to be certain we have it in our minds.

Consider this scenario.

Tourist: Excuse me, could you direct me to a place called the Chocolate Fetish?

Local: Sure, right now you are on Biltmore Avenue. So what you want to do is go up this hill to the square where you see the tall monument there in the middle. Just cross over Biltmore at the square. You will be walking toward a restaurant called Rhubarb. When you get across the street, head to your right. You'll see the BB&T building. You can't miss it. It's the tallest building in town, and it's sheathed in dark gray glass. Head toward the BB&T building, and turn left on that corner. That's Patton Avenue. Walk three blocks on Patton. You'll come to Lexington, and you'll see the old Kress building; it's a gallery now. Cross Lexington and continue walking on Patton. You'll pass several shops, and you'll see a left-turn-only street; that's Church. Continue walking until you get to Haywood. On that corner you'll see Pritchard Park in front of you. The Wells Fargo building will be on your right, and across the street on your left is the old S&W building. Now cross over Haywood as if you are going to the park, then turn to the right and go up Haywood. You'll cross over College Street. There's a restaurant called Mayfel's on that corner. Walk on to the next street, and you'll pass two clothing stores and a wig shop. You can't miss the wig shop—there are all colors of wigs in the windows there. So now you'll cross over Battery Park, and you'll see a restaurant called Isa. You're still on Haywood, and you will pass Isa and a boutique and the entrance to a courtyard and the next store will be Chocolate Fetish on your left. Got it?

Tourist: So let me make sure I have it. Walk up to the square. Cross Biltmore. Cross Patton and turn left. Cross Lexington. Cross Haywood and turn right. Cross College and Battery Park. Then it's the third business on the left.

Local: Exactly. You've got it.

Let's think about what happened here. The tourist needed directions to reach a destination; she had a purpose, and she sought out the information. The local understood the tourist is unfamiliar with the area (had limited background knowledge) and wanted to give as many specific, concrete examples as he could provide (perhaps too much). The tourist listened for the significant details she would need to reach her destination. She actively listened, holding on to each significant detail. When the local finished with his description, the tourist *summarized* the information and condensed it to the most essential bits needed for her purpose.

Proficient readers do this as well. Proficient readers approach the text with some intention that guides their attention in a particular direction. The particulars they focus on will be determined by the intentions they bring to the text. *Summary* asks the student for a condensed essence of the text. The reader's task, then, is to reduce the text to essential bits and to restate them as succinctly as possible. We summarize to generate a more manageable version of the information.

While summarizing is something that people do naturally in the world beyond school, we find it helpful to make students conscious of it. Our task, as we see it, is to connect the thinking children do outside of school with the act of reading while in school. We believe it makes sense to begin with summarizing daily life events to demonstrate why a summary is helpful and how one chooses what to include, that is, to help students understand a summary is simply a condensed version of the most significant details.

Consider exploring with your students the situations in daily life where we pause and summarize to help us make sense and retain essential information.

- ✦ Revisiting the rules of a game
- ✦ Recounting the steps of an event
- ✦ Reporting the highlights of a game or event
- ✦ Directions

- Recipes
- Dismissal procedures
- Fire drill/emergency procedures
- Library checkout and other school routines

⊡ LESSON FOCUS Introduce the Concept of Summarizing

Readers, I'd like you to think about the time we spend during lunch at school. Think about everything we do to get ready for lunch before we leave the room. Think about how we get from here to the lunchroom and everything we have to do before we sit down at our table. Think about what we have to remember while we are having lunch and all the things we do before leaving the lunchroom to return to our classroom.

Sit with those thoughts. Recall as much detail as you can.

[Pause briefly.]

Talk with your partner and share your thoughts.

[Pause briefly while they buzz, trying to recall details of the lunch routine.]

Readers, let me hear from you. I'll make a list here as you share what you recalled.

[As they talk, chart the details in chronological order.]

[It may look something like this:]

After science the teacher tells us to put away our materials and tells group 1 to go wash their hands. Then group 1 goes back to their seats to wait. Kids who brought their lunch pick it up from the counter. Then group 2 goes to wash their hands. When they finish group 2 kids get their lunch boxes if they brought lunch. When group 2 sits down to wait, then group 3 goes to wash their hands. When they finish and pick up their lunch if they brought one, then everyone lines up at the door. The teacher opens the door, and the line leader walks at the front of the line and the teacher walks in the middle. We all walk down the hall and turn left at the end of the hall, go past the custodian's closet, and then turn right to go into the lunchroom. Usually we have to wait in line while Mrs. Tucker's class gets their food. When we get up to the front we pick up a tray (if we didn't bring a lunch from home), and we tell the lunch ladies what we want on our trays. Then we walk to the back of the cafeteria. Our table is the third one from the back wall. The first person in line goes to the end of the table, puts the tray down and sits. We eat lunch and talk quietly to the people near us. We don't shout to people down the table, and we don't trade food. After we are finished we wait in our place until the teacher stands up. Then we all stand up, and the person at the end of the table leads the line down to the trash cans where we dump the food we didn't eat. Then we put our trays in the window on the conveyor belt, and it takes the dirty trays to the dishwasher. Then we follow the line leader down the hall and back to the classroom. If you have a lunchbox or bag, you put it away. We go to our seats, and the teacher reads to us before starting social studies.

Readers, that is a lot of detail, isn't it? What if we needed a short list to remind us about only the most important details? Let's imagine that we have to make directions for lunch that will fit on one side of this card [hold up a 4 × 6 index card]. Think about what you'd write on the card.

Review the details we collected and sit with your thoughts for a bit.

[Pause as they review and think.]

Readers, talk with your partner to decide what you would write on a short list for someone who had never been to lunch at school.

[Pause while they negotiate their ideas.]

I'll start the summary list with "Wash your hands."

Let's attempt to keep the list to the most important information.

Your list may look something like this:

- Wash your hands.
- Line up.
- Walk to the lunchroom.
- Go through the line and get your lunch.
- Sit down and eat.
- Empty your tray.
- Line up.
- Walk back to class.
- Get ready for social studies.

Readers, take a moment to examine our list. Notice how the list is different from the collection of details. Think about which one would help you remember what to do. Why is one easier than the other?

[Pause for some brief and focused dialog.]

So we took the longer, more detailed text and summarized it to include only the most important parts. We searched for the ideas that we need to get our task done, and we summarized the text to make a list of the most important parts. The summary would be enough to remind us.

I'd like you to tuck this away in your memory. When we are reading it is very helpful to pause from time to time and make a short list—to summarize—what you want to hold on to.

Tomorrow we will revisit this idea with a story everyone knows.

⬅️ LESSON FOCUS Exploring Opportunities to Summarize as Readers

Readers, recently we sat together and talked about summarizing. We thought about times when we need to make a short list or summary to help us remember what is important.

Today we are going to revisit a best friend book, *Fireflies!* by Julie Brinckloe. We have done a lot of thinking with this book, but today I'm going to read through without stopping until we get to the last page.

[Hold the book up face out.]

When I turn the last page I'll ask you to think about the most important parts with your partner and make a summary of the story. Let's get started.

[Open the book with the text and illustrations facing out. Remember, this is a very familiar book, one you have read aloud many times. Read the entire text with expression and pacing that matches the tone and mood of the story.]

Every time we read this book I just smile. It's one of my favorites. Readers, turn now to your partner, and decide what is most important to remember about *Fireflies!*

[Pause briefly as they negotiate ideas.]

As you share, I'll jot your thoughts on the chart.

[Jot the ideas as they are presented without regard to sequence. It may look something like Chart 1 on the next page.]

Readers, we have a list of events, but we need to get them in the order they happen in the story. Take a look at the list and talk with your partner about which one should be first.

[Pause briefly to allow them time to work out the order.]

Readers, let's put these in order.

[As they determine order, jot a numeral next to each item in the list (see Chart 2). You may have to scratch out a few and adjust as they move through.]

Let's work together to make a summary from our list.

[Lead an interactive writing experience to develop a short paragraph from the list that will result in a cohesive summary.]

The boy wanted to catch fireflies. His parents said yes. He got a jar, punched holes in the top, and ran outside. He caught hundreds of fireflies and brought them inside. He kept the jar next to his bed and watched fireflies blink on and off. They stopped glowing, and he felt really bad. He walked to his window and opened the jar. The fireflies flew out into the air and began to blink again. He cried because he almost killed them.

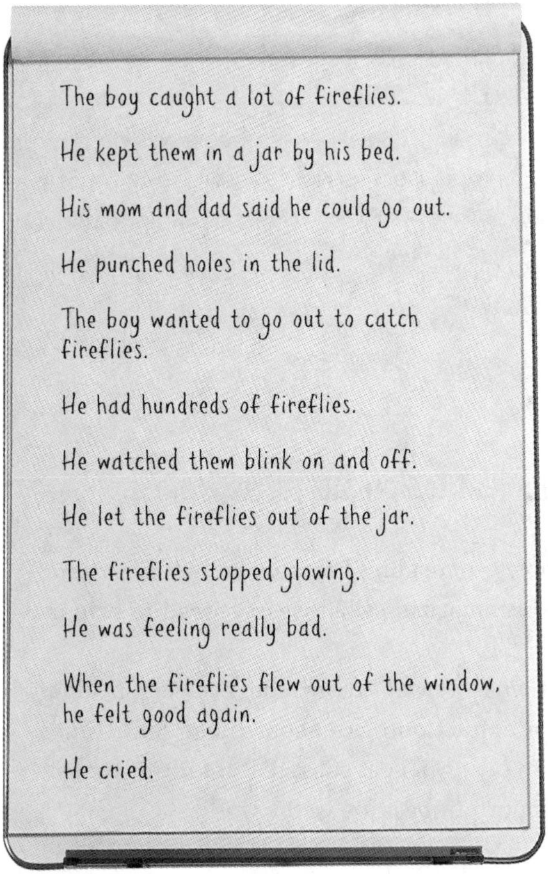

The boy caught a lot of fireflies.

He kept them in a jar by his bed.

His mom and dad said he could go out.

He punched holes in the lid.

The boy wanted to go out to catch fireflies.

He had hundreds of fireflies.

He watched them blink on and off.

He let the fireflies out of the jar.

The fireflies stopped glowing.

He was feeling really bad.

When the fireflies flew out of the window, he felt good again.

He cried.

Chart 1

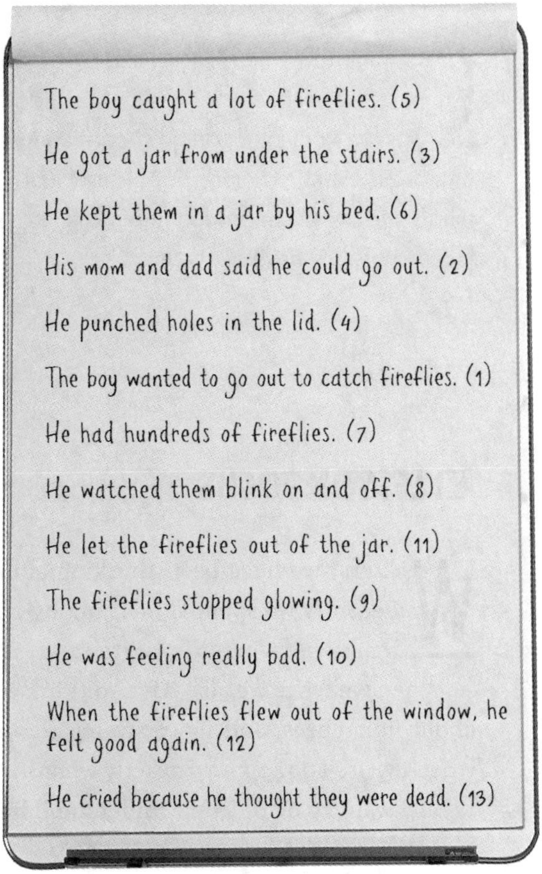

The boy caught a lot of fireflies. (5)

He got a jar from under the stairs. (3)

He kept them in a jar by his bed. (6)

His mom and dad said he could go out. (2)

He punched holes in the lid. (4)

The boy wanted to go out to catch fireflies. (1)

He had hundreds of fireflies. (7)

He watched them blink on and off. (8)

He let the fireflies out of the jar. (11)

The fireflies stopped glowing. (9)

He was feeling really bad. (10)

When the fireflies flew out of the window, he felt good again. (12)

He cried because he thought they were dead. (13)

Chart 2

[Read the summary together and confirm that the important details have been captured.]

Readers, now we have a summary of *Fireflies!* by Julie Brinckloe. Our summary will help us remember the story. Summarizing is an important way to hold on to the important information when we need to remember what we read. Sometimes we wait until the very end of the text before we summarize. If there is a lot to remember, it can be helpful to summarize each section or chapter.

As you move out to reading today, try summarizing what you read. Think about the important parts, and try saying those in a short paragraph to yourself. You may find it helpful to write the brief summary on sticky notes for each segment.

Flip It from Reading to Writing

Consider how writers think in the preparation and production of their work. Writers often begin with a small bit and grow it into an idea for a text. It may be a character sketch, or a strong opinion on a topic, an overheard conversation, or a family story. Writers begin with an idea, character, event, opinion, or an argument that will propel them forward. Writing a brief planning summary, a condensed prewriting of the essence of their intentions, can help writers remain focused as they develop the text.

►◫ LESSON FOCUS Exploring Opportunities to Summarize as Writers

Writers, we have been thinking about how our reading helps us be better writers. Recently we spent time thinking about summarizing what we have read to help us remember what is important.

When we write we also have to think about what we want to include. I've been reading about honeybees, and I'm planning to write a nonfiction piece about them. Sometimes when I write I don't know exactly what I want to say until I get started. But for this project I really want to help people understand how important bees are to the world.

I'm thinking it would help me get focused if I summarize the ideas I may want to include when I write. I remember that we began with a list when we made a summary of *Fireflies!* Then we put them in order and wrote a paragraph.

So, last night I decided to try that in my notebook. Take a look at this page. [See Figure 7.1.] [Show the page from your notebook.]

After I made a list of important facts to include, I decided to write it all in a quick paragraph like we did in reading. [See Figure 7.2.] [Show the second page from your notebook.]

One way I can think about what is important as I am writing is to think about what the summary would look like when my reader is finished. This is a different way of thinking about summarizing, isn't it? This kind of summary is like a plan. Now I'm ready to begin my draft. Writers, today you are beginning a nonfiction piece. You may want to try what I did and begin with a list of important facts. Then, write those facts into one brief summary paragraph that will help you stay focused.

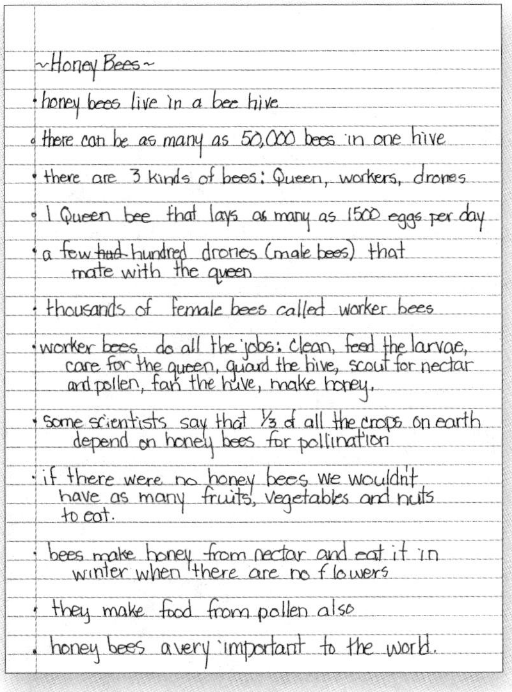

~Honey Bees~
· honey bees live in a bee hive
· there can be as many as 50,000 bees in one hive
· there are 3 kinds of bees: Queen, workers, drones
· 1 Queen bee that lays as many as 1500 eggs per day
· a few hundred drones (male bees) that mate with the queen
· thousands of female bees called worker bees
· worker bees do all the jobs: clean, feed the larvae, care for the queen, guard the hive, scout for nectar and pollen, fan the hive, make honey.
· some scientists say that ⅓ of all the crops on earth depend on honey bees for pollination
· if there were no honey bees we wouldn't have as many fruits, vegetables and nuts to eat.
· bees make honey from nectar and eat it in winter when there are no flowers
· they make food from pollen also
· honey bees a very important to the world.

Figure 7.1 Honeybee Facts

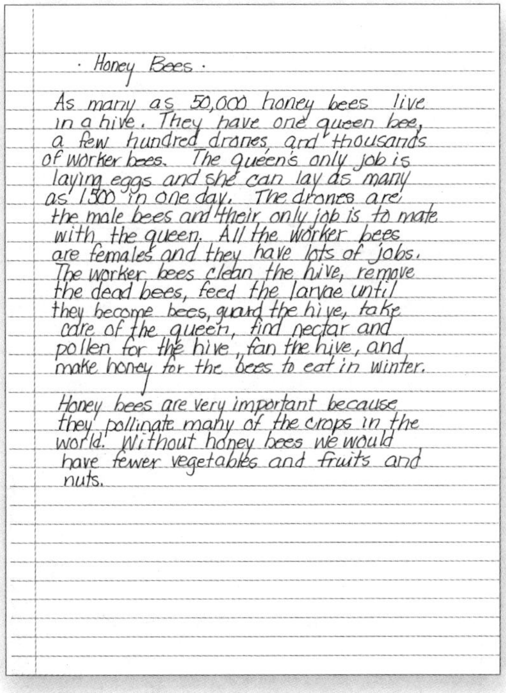

· Honey Bees ·
As many as 50,000 honey bees live in a hive. They have one queen bee, a few hundred drones, and thousands of worker bees. The queen's only job is laying eggs and she can lay as many as 1500 in one day. The drones are the male bees and their only job is to mate with the queen. All the worker bees are females and they have lots of jobs. The worker bees clean the hive, remove the dead bees, feed the larvae until they become bees, guard the hive, take care of the queen, find nectar and pollen for the hive, fan the hive, and make honey for the bees to eat in winter.

Honey bees are very important because they pollinate many of the crops in the world. Without honey bees we would have fewer vegetables and fruits and nuts.

Figure 7.2 Honeybees Paragraph

Writing Samples

These two samples from Cruz show how he began a "Where I'm From" poem with a summary of the information he wanted to include. For this poem he began with categories that would become stanzas in the poem. The poem follows his summary/plan sheet (see Figures 7.3a and 7.3b).

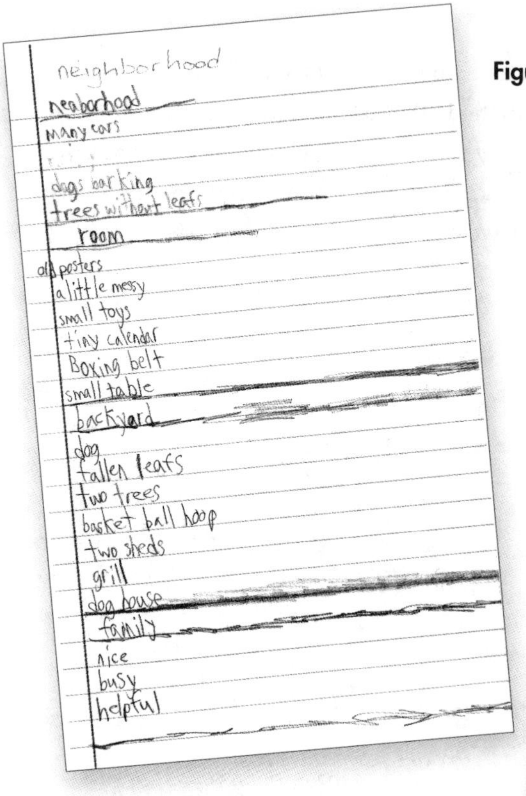

Figure 7.3a Cruz, Fifth Grade (Poem Categories)

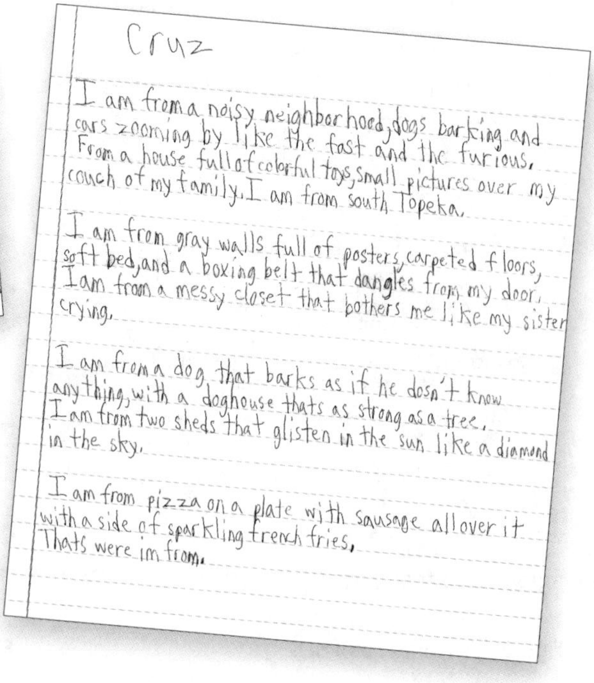

neighborhood

neabarhood
Many cars

dogs barking
trees with hart leafs
room

old posters
a little messy
small toys
tiny calender
Boxing belt
small table
backyard

dog
fallen leafs
two trees
basket ball hoop
two sheds
grill
dog house
family

nice
busy
helpful

Cruz

I am from a noisy neighborhood, dogs barking and cars zooming by like the fast and the furious, From a house full of colorful toys, small pictures over my couch of my family. I am from south Topeka.

I am from gray walls full of posters, carpeted floors, soft bed, and a boxing belt that dangles from my door, I am from a messy closet that bothers me like my sister crying.

I am from a dog that barks as if he dosn't know anything, with a doghouse thats as strong as a tree, I am from two sheds that glisten in the sun like a diamond in the sky.

I am from pizza on a plate with sausage all over it with a side of sparkling french fries, Thats were im from.

Figure 7.3b Cruz, Fifth Grade (Poem)

Additional Texts: Summarizing

All About Frogs by Jim Arnosky: Arnosky provides younger readers with a text to invite them to summarize as they read. Each page is rich in facts about frogs, their habitats, and what they need to survive.

Birmingham Sunday by Larry Dane Brimner: This book is a dense text about the 1963 bombing of the 16th Street Baptist Church in Birmingham, Alabama. Every page offers detailed information that may require readers to stop and summarize to avoid gaps in understanding.

The Emperor's Egg by Martin Jenkins: This book offers information within a visually supportive text. The text is broken into segments describing the role each penguin parent plays in the birth of a baby penguin. There are opportunities to summarize after each segment.

Mother to Tigers by George Ella Lyon: Helen Delaney Martini helped workers at the Bronx Zoo by becoming a nurse for baby tigers that were too little to survive without constant care. She was the first to bring abandoned tiger babies home and the first to save an abandoned cub. Throughout the story, information is given about her nurturing, including how she fed, bathed, and cared for these wild babies.

8

SYNTHESIZING

Reba has a cabin out in the country near her childhood home. The cabin is her escape place, and the drive from her home in Decatur takes about three and a half hours. She makes this trip on a regular basis and knows the route very well. But she sometimes gets caught in traffic jams on I-65 or US-280 due to road construction, accidents, or heavy traffic heading into or out of Birmingham on weekends. On a few occasions her GPS has rerouted her off the interstate and onto two-lane highways that run parallel to the interstate through small towns. Over time Reba has learned to read the traffic patterns as she drives. When she sees the volume increase or vehicles slowing in particular spots, she considers the options she has for getting off the interstate and onto one of the smaller highways. She draws upon her experiences with traffic patterns, road construction, and alternate routes; she assesses current road conditions and makes a decision. In these situations Reba weaves current information with her prior knowledge and arrives at a decision about the best option to move her forward. In short, she synthesizes information she gathers during the drive to make sense of the current situation and generate a plan of action.

Synthesis asks for a contribution from the reader. It isn't satisfied with condensing and restating the essence of the text. Synthesis expects the reader to do more, to make the text personal and relevant, to weave a more robust tapestry than the text itself has presented. Synthesis expects the reader to leave the text with more than he found on the page. Synthesis is like weaving. We have threads from the text and threads from our lives that we are weaving together as we read. We may also pull from our inferences and summaries in the process of weaving meaning. The tapestry of meaning evolves during the process of reading and continues to evolve even after we have left the text. While we reflect on what we have read, engage in dialog with others about the text, or write in response to our reading, we continue weaving meaning. As our understanding evolves we may change our minds and move in a different direction. But each bit along the way is woven in until we arrive at a satisfactory conclusion. Each reader will weave a personal tapestry and make personal meaning. There will be similarities from reader to reader; after all, the threads from the text remain constant. However, the threads brought by each reader may differ, resulting in variations of meaning woven by each reader. By definition synthesis results in something new, something more than what was.

Synthesis occurs in the world outside school and beyond the act of reading. When we weave our existing insights with experience over time to make new meaning, we are synthesizing. Synthesis draws upon what we have available in the moment and continues to evolve as we move forward, bringing in new threads of thought and experience.

⊞ LESSON FOCUS Introduce the Concept of Synthesizing

Readers, sometimes we understand something quickly and can make a decision right away. Then, other times we get only a little information at a time, and we have to wait until we have enough to decide.

Imagine you are standing on first base and your friend is up to bat. You know you may need to run to second base, but you wait to get more information before deciding. First you scan the field and notice you have a teammate on third base. There is no one on second. You know you will have to run to second if your friend gets a hit. You know your teammate on third could stand still or make a run for home. You know if your friend gets the hit he will have to run for first. You have all that information from checking the field.

And because you play baseball you have some background knowledge. You know the opposing team will try to get as many outs as possible, and they will try to keep your third-base teammate from making it to home plate. So you stand on first, ready to run. You know you could try to steal second, but you'd have to time that just right or you could cost your team an out.

Standing there on first base with all that information zooming around in your head, trying to weave it all into a clear decision, is one way we synthesize in our lives outside school.

In that baseball game you have information about the game because you play baseball frequently. That's your background knowledge. You understand the rules, how the field is set up, and which way to run. You can picture that in your mind because you have schema for how baseball works. You are standing on base and taking in all the information available from the field, from your background, from your schema and you watch your friend who is up to bat. At the right moment you weave all that information together and make the decision to make a run for second base.

We do that in reading as well. When we choose a book, we think about the topic and what we know. We think about the type of text. Is it a story or a poem? Is it an information book or an article? Is it an essay or an ABC book? That helps us know what to expect and how the information will be presented. We begin to read and get bits of information. As we read along we add more information, and our thoughts may change a bit. We may question something the author presents. We pause along the way and summarize what we've read so far. We think about what may come next. And we read more. By the time we have read to the end we have woven all those ideas together and have a new understanding. That is synthesizing, or weaving all of the information together into some new insights and thoughts.

⊟ LESSON FOCUS   Introduce the Concept of Synthesizing as Readers

Readers, we have been exploring what it means to synthesize when we read. Today I've chosen a book you have not seen in our class this year. It is called *Seven Blind Mice*, and it is written and illustrated by Ed Young. In this book, one character synthesizes information to create meaning. Think about that as I read this short book from the first page to the last without stopping. When we reach the end I will pause and ask you to think and share your thoughts.

[Hold the book face out, and read the title and author/illustrator. Read the book from start to finish in a slow, deliberate, and even tone.]

Readers, let's pause here for a moment. Sit with this story in your mind and think about which character synthesized information. Reflect on how that thinking made a difference in the meaning for all the mice.

[Pause briefly.]

Share your thinking with your partner.

[Pause briefly.]

Readers, let me hear from a few of you. What did you and your partner notice?

[Listen as a few students share thoughts. Their comments may be similar to these:

- ✦ White Mouse synthesized information because she listened to each of the other mice.

- ✦ White Mouse added each part to her thinking before deciding.

- ✦ White Mouse waited until she had all the information so she knew there was more than just one part.

- ✦ White Mouse explored the whole elephant because she listened and thought about all the different parts each of the other mice told about.]

Think with me for a moment. We all agree that White Mouse is the one who synthesized information and that helped her understand and make meaning. So talk with me about why the other mice, like the fourth and fifth and sixth mouse, didn't do the same thing.

[Pause briefly.]

Let's take a moment now to think through how that happened. Let me hear your thoughts. [Student comments will vary, but may include statements such as these:

- ✦ All the other mice explored only one part.

- ✦ Each mouse believed the part he found was all of it, the whole thing, so he made a decision without all the information.

- ✦ Those mice who went later, like the fifth mouse, could have made better decisions if they had been listening and thinking about all the parts.

- ✦ The other mice believed they didn't need more information. They didn't listen and think about how all the information adds up. Only White Mouse did that.]

So, readers, let's take a lesson from this story. When we are reading we need to keep an open mind and expect the writer to give us more information as we move along. Then we need to be like White Mouse and think about all the information before making a final decision.

Readers, recently we read *Seven Blind Mice* by Ed Young. We explored how White Mouse synthesized information brought back from all the other mice and came to the conclusion that the new something was an elephant.

Today we are going to be like White Mouse. I'm going to read a few pages from three different books. [Show the cover of each book as you name it.]

1. *Are You a Bee?* by Judy Allen

2. *Honey in a Hive* by Anne Rockwell

3. *The Honey Makers* by Gail Gibbons

I am going to read only the pages that give information about gathering nectar and pollen and making honey. I'll pause after reading each new section for us to summarize what we heard from each author. As I read from each of these authors, I want you to think like White Mouse. Keep your mind open and synthesize the information.

[Hold up *Are You a Bee?*]

Readers, the first book is titled *Are You a Bee?* by Judy Allen. Remember, I am going to read only those pages with information about gathering pollen and nectar and making honey.

[Open the book to page 16 and read pages 16 through 18.]

Readers, let's pause here and make note of what we know so far. I'll write information from Judy Allen in blue.

[Pause briefly for them to reflect and respond. Use a blue marker and make a bulleted list.]

- Nectar is a sweet liquid.

- Nectar is inside the flower.

- Honeybees have a long tongue that helps them reach the nectar.

- Honeybees have a special stomach to carry nectar.

- When they are in the flower they get covered in pollen.

- Honeybees scrape the pollen off their bodies with their front legs and put it in pollen baskets on their back legs.

- Other worker bees in the hive help put the pollen and nectar into empty cells.

- Honeybees mix nectar and pollen to make beebread.

- Nectar stored in the cells will turn into honey.

Readers, we have some information about honeybees gathering nectar and pollen and making honey.

[Show the cover of the second book.]

Let's read the information in *Honey in a Hive*, and think about the new information we get from Anne Rockwell.

I'm going to page 16 where Anne Rockwell explains how worker bees find the flowers, gather the nectar and pollen, and make honey.

[Open the book to page 16 and read to the end of page 19.]

Now we have additional information. Pause a moment to think about any new information we can add from Anne Rockwell.

[Pause briefly.]

Readers, take a look at our list. Talk with your partner and decide what new information we can add.

[Allow time for them to think and talk with partners.]

Let me hear what you noticed. I'll jot the information from Anne Rockwell in green.

[Pause while they add new information. Extend the bulleted list.]

- One bee can carry only a little nectar or pollen.
- Honeybees use a dance to tell other bees where to find the flowers.
- It takes many bees to bring nectar and pollen to the hive.
- Honeybees have to make lots of trips to the flowers to get enough nectar and pollen.
- It takes a lot of nectar to make a little bit of honey.
- Bees put the nectar in a cell in the hive.
- A cell has six sides, and it's made of wax.
- Some bees fly out to get more nectar.
- Other bees stay in the hive and fan the nectar with their wings.
- The nectar is watery; when the bees fan it, the nectar becomes thick and sticky.
- The nectar becomes honey.
- When a cell is filled with honey, worker bees seal the top with wax.

So we have additional information that provides us with more detail and more facts to help us understand how bees gather and use nectar and pollen. Let's take a look at one more book, *The Honey Makers* by Gail Gibbons.

[Present the cover.]

Readers, I've flagged the pages with information about gathering and using nectar and pollen. Let's take a look.

[The pages in this book are not numbered. Open to the spread with a diagram featuring an outline of the bee with the "crop" or "honey stomach" labeled. The diagram is in the upper-left corner. Read the text on this spread and the next two spreads, ending with information on "Dances of the Honeybees."]

Let's pause a moment to think about what we have just heard from Gail Gibbons. What additional information should we add to our growing list? You will find it helpful to look back at our list and think about what we have learned from Judy Allen and Anne Rockwell.

[Pause briefly to let them sit with these ideas and zero in on specific additions.]

Now turn to your partner and decide what we should add to our list.

[Pause long enough for partners to work out what is new information.]

Readers, let me hear what you have decided. I'll add the new information from Gail Gibbons in red.

[Add new information in red marker.]

- Honeybees collect nectar with their proboscis.
- She stores nectar in a special part of her stomach called the crop or the honey stomach.
- Some pollen is collected in baskets on the bee's hind legs.
- After a bee visits lots of flowers the worker bee's honey stomach is full of nectar and she returns to the hive.
- When the bees are back in the hive they vomit the nectar from their honey stomach and pass it along to other bees with their tongue.
- The bees pass the nectar from one bee to the next until some of the moisture is gone.
- They put the nectar into a honey cell.
- They fill more cells with nectar and seal them with wax.
- Worker bees, called house bees, fan their wings to evaporate more moisture.
- Other worker bees put a wax seal over the top of the cell.
- The nectar becomes honey.
- A honeybee can go to 10,000 flowers in one day.

◆ The nectar collected by one honeybee in a lifetime makes only one teaspoon of honey.

Readers, right now we are like White Mouse in *Seven Blind Mice*. We have heard information from three different authors. All three of them—Judy Allen, Anne Rockwell, and Gail Gibbons—are reporting on honeybees and how honeybees gather and use nectar and pollen. Each of them gives us information that adds to our understanding. But when we think like White Mouse and weave all that information together, we know more about honeybees.

Pause for a moment and read over our list. As you do, think about how we might weave that information together to explain how honeybees gather and use nectar and pollen. Sit with those thoughts.

[Pause briefly as they read and think.]

Now turn to your partners and try composing a couple of statements that include information from each author.

[Allow time for them to think together and draft a few statements in their notebooks.]

Readers, let's hear from a few of you.

   ◆ Nectar is a sweet, watery liquid found inside a flower. Nectar becomes sticky and thick honey when the moisture is evaporated from it.

   ◆ A honeybee collects nectar with her proboscis, which is a long tongue that can reach down into the flower. She has a special honey stomach called a crop where she stores the nectar she is taking back to the hive.

   ◆ A honeybee will visit several flowers, collecting nectar with her proboscis, before her crop is full.

   ◆ Honeybees have little hairs on their bodies, and pollen collects on those hairs. The honeybees use their front legs to scrape the pollen off their bodies and store it in special pollen baskets formed by tiny hairs on their back legs.

   ◆ Some pollen stays on their bodies, and that pollen gets spread from one flower to another. This is called pollination and helps plants grow seeds.

   ◆ Since one honeybee can carry only a little nectar and pollen back to the hive, it takes lots of bees making many trips from the hive to the flowers to gather enough nectar and pollen to fill the cells and make honey. The honeybees do a special dance to tell other honeybees in the hive where they can find the flowers with nectar.

Readers, we are thinking like White Mouse. Just like White Mouse we are taking information from each of the three books and synthesizing that information into statements that tell more. As I read your statements I'm noticing that you are also weaving in information we didn't include on our list.

Today as you move out into your reading I'd like you to try thinking like White Mouse. Think about the information you gather, and weave it together with what you know. Notice how that makes reading even more meaningful.

Flip It from Reading to Writing

Writers engage with the texts of their lives and with life experiences. It is through this attention that they begin weaving the threads of thought that will lead them to the need to share that thinking, insights, or stories. The text a writer will construct is not something that fell into her mind as a complete whole. Instead it is a construction, a fabric woven from the threads of previous experiences, prior knowledge, and some present trigger that prompted the action. It is a synthesis of experiences, thoughts, and language. The product emerging from the efforts of a writer is the result of synthesis, something new woven from the fibers of life. Even if she has a plan, an image of the whole, she is weaving a tapestry as she writes. The end result is a synthesis of her thoughts and language, her intentions and understandings.

◀ LESSON FOCUS Exploring Opportunities to Synthesize as Writers

Writers, we have been exploring what it means to synthesize when we are reading. You may remember White Mouse in the book *Seven Blind Mice* by Ed Young. Let's think of her for a moment. White Mouse sat quietly listening and thinking and gathering information while each of the other six mice went out to explore. In the story, each of the other mice explored only one part of the elephant, and when each returned he gave a report on that one part only. Each mouse had only one small bit to share. But White Mouse sat quietly and listened as each of the other mice went out and returned with a report. She listened to each report and began to add it all together. Before White Mouse went out she had all the reports from the other mice in her mind. She took all that information with her as she set out to explore all the parts of the new something. When she returned she was able to give a more complete report about the new something, which was, of course, the elephant.

Today we are going to explore how synthesizing helps writers generate more complete texts. Writers also need to think like White Mouse. We think about our own experiences and jot down the ideas we want to include. We think about questions we have and questions our readers may have. We may even write those questions in our notebooks. We search out information to help us answer those. We read what other writers have done and make notes about ideas that can make our texts more complete. We examine how other writers presented information and think about craft and structure as we draft our own writing.

Writers, think back to the day I read a few pages from three different books about honeybees. That day we read only those pages with information about how honeybees gather and use nectar and pollen. After I read from each book you helped me make a list of the important facts. Then we reviewed the information and made a list that synthesized all the bits from each book. That day we were readers thinking like White Mouse as our minds took in more and more information.

But we were also writers thinking like White Mouse. We read three different reports to make one new list with more complete information. We wrote that list, and we could use it to begin a new piece on honeybees.

Remember, I've been working on a nonfiction piece, and I want to help my readers know how important honeybees are in the world. As I get ready to write, our list will be helpful because it can help me explain how honey is made. I can begin with that list, but to write the whole piece I will need more information about honeybees.

So I'm going to have to think like White Mouse. First I think about what I already know. I have a list in my notebook that I showed to you when we explored how readers and writers use summarizing to make meaning. That list is my starting point.

Last night as I was thinking about my project, I made a list of things I need to explore (see Figure 8.1). I'll use this list to help me gather other texts to read. Then, before I write my draft, I'll make notes from each text and synthesize all that information like White Mouse did.

As I'm reading to grow my knowledge I'll also notice how writers use charts and labels and diagrams and headings. That will help me get organized. When I'm ready to begin my draft, I'll have a lot of information tucked away in my mind just like White Mouse. I have a lot of work to do.

Writers, we have been gathering information for our nonfiction projects. Today as you move back to your writing spot I'd like you to think like White Mouse. Pause a

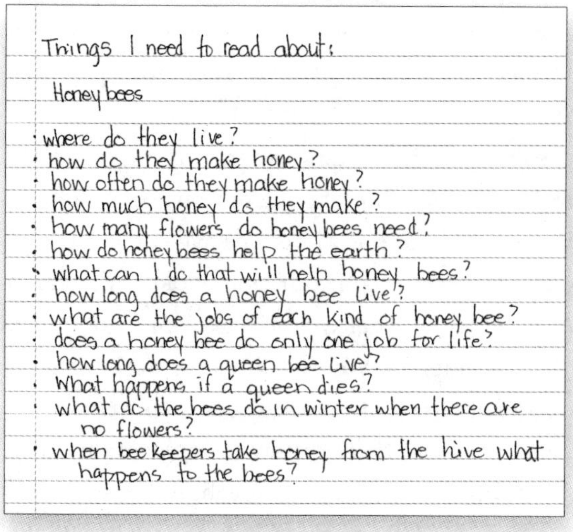

Figure 8.1 Things I Need to Explore

> Things I need to read about:
>
> Honey bees
>
> • where do they live?
> • how do they make honey?
> • how often do they make honey?
> • how much honey do they make?
> • how many flowers do honey bees need?
> • how do honey bees help the earth?
> • what can I do that will help honey bees?
> • how long does a honey bee live?
> • what are the jobs of each kind of honey bee?
> • does a honey bee do only one job for life?
> • how long does a queen bee live?
> • what happens if a queen dies?
> • what do the bees do in winter when there are no flowers?
> • when bee keepers take honey from the hive what happens to the bees?

moment to think about what you already know. Make some notes about that in your notebook. Then take a moment to make a list of what you need to explore and read more about. Let's spend some time today gathering information from three sources and making notes for our projects.

Writing Sample

Aaliyah has developed a keen interest in dolphins. While thinking about this topic she generates a list of questions that will guide her focus (see Figure 8.2).

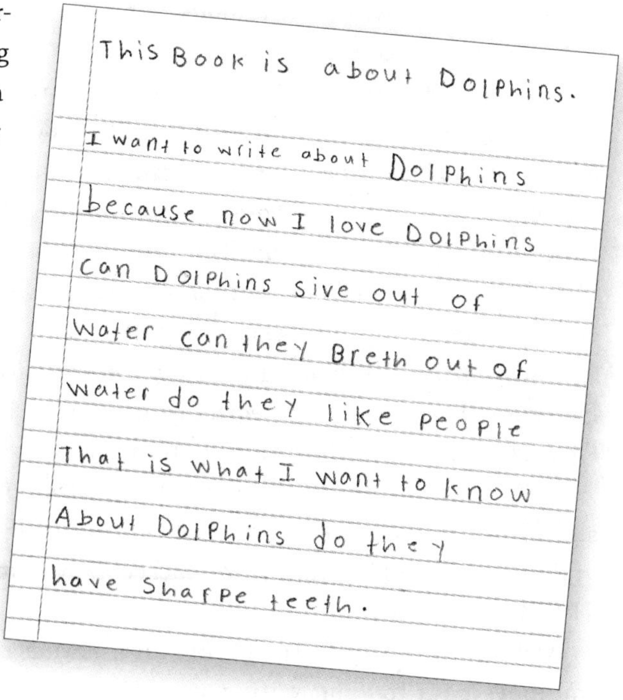

Figure 8.2 Aaliyah, Third Grade (ELL student)

> This Book is about Dolphins.
>
> I want to write about Dolphins because now I love Dolphins
>
> can Dolphins sive out of water con they Breth out of water do they like people
>
> That is what I want to know About Dolphins do they have Sharpe teeth.

Additional Texts: Synthesizing

Freedom Summer by Deborah Wiles: This story takes place in the 1960s as the civil rights movement was making its mark on America. Two boys—one black and one white—are friends who play and swim together in the local creek but long to swim together in the town's pool. After the desegregation law is passed, Joe and John Henry rush to the pool for their first swim, but once there they witness the pool being filled in with tar to prevent blacks and whites from swimming together. This story will be meaningful to children who may have limited background of this era of history and will help them better understand human rights issues and the feelings that can result from rejection. New understandings will emerge from discussions about this book.

Smoky Nights by Eve Bunting: This is the story of the LA riots told from the perspective of a young boy and his mother who are living in an apartment above the street where people are setting fires, looting stores, and destroying everything in sight. The book gives children the opportunity to discuss what Bunting describes and merge it with what they know from the news of the day to form a new understanding of how riots occur. The book gives readers an insight into the behavior of those participating in the riots as explained by someone who witnessed the events.

Twenty-One Elephants and Still Standing by April Jones Prince: Prince offers readers a history into the fourteen years of the construction of the Brooklyn Bridge and the fears of some who questioned if it would be safe for traveling. The year was 1883 and no bridge of this magnitude had ever been built. To prove a point, P.T. Barnum, creator of "The Greatest Show on Earth," staged his greatest performance soon after the bridge was completed. He lined up all twenty-one of his elephants and paraded them through the streets of New York City. Much to everyone's delight, he then marched them one by one across the Brooklyn Bridge, which was still standing after the march of the elephants. Children will marvel at this book because, for them, bridges like this have always been around and the safety of crossing them has never been an issue. So the synthesis will involve merging this new information with what they already know about bridges and the size and weight of elephants.

9

VISUALIZING

Most of us have made a list of things we need at the market before setting off on a shopping trip. Perhaps while making the list you think about how the market is laid out and where items will be located in the store. Perhaps you've had the experience of getting there only to realize you left that list on the kitchen counter. So you move through the store and try to recall the list. You try to see the pantry, the refrigerator, and freezer and images of what needs to be replaced. Or maybe you call up images of the list itself as you move through the market pushing the cart.

We know what it means to visualize. We do it several times a day. We visualize when we try to recall where we left the keys. We visualize when we are stressed and try to take our minds to someplace peaceful. We visualize when we are lost in thought about some future event we are looking forward to. We visualize about those things we dread. Visualization is an ordinary function of the human brain.

Remind yourself and your students that the strategies we use to make meaning from our reading and bring meaning to our writing come from the ordinary things we do each day to make sense of our lives.

When we visualize we pull up images from our experiences. Perhaps you are buying a new lamp to replace one the dog knocked off the table in the den. While shopping you likely visualize the space and consider the style and size of the lamp before making a selection. Because it is a space you know very well, you find it easy to visualize. Other situations may push us to construct an image from bits and pieces stored away. Perhaps you've been asked to speak at an event that you've never attended. You try to visualize the location, the school, and the people. You try to construct an image in your mind from your own experiences. You visualize in an effort to bring a bit of clarity, to reduce the anxiety of the unknown, or to float on the excitement. You visualize naturally, perhaps even unconsciously.

⊞ LESSON FOCUS Introduce the Concept of Visualizing

R eaders, let's take a moment to think about something we all know. Pause for a moment and think about our playground, just as it is right now. Think about the equipment we have to play on. Think about your favorite spot. Think about things that have made us laugh out there. Think about your best memory on the playground.

Let's sit with those thoughts for a few seconds. Just think and hold the images in your head. [Pause briefly, and sit in silence.]

I'm seeing the swings move back and forth. I can hear that sound they make when they move, that creaking sound and the way the chains rattle. I'm hearing the kids laughing and talking, and I am seeing their jackets flying in the wind. What are you seeing in your mind?

[Proceed, allowing a few children to talk about the images they are holding in their minds.]

Let's pause a moment. Turn to your partner, and share what you were seeing. Remember, when it is your turn to listen, try to see in your mind what your partner describes to you.

[Allow a brief time for them to share. Offer some summary statement.]

Readers, let's pause here. It's wonderful that our minds can remember things like sounds and images from our past. When we stop to think about those things and try to recall them, we can picture ourselves back in those places. When we do that it is called visualizing.

We can visualize to help us remember something and to help us make sense. I'm going to read a story about a mouse named Frederick. It is written and illustrated by Leo Lionni. As I read I invite you to think about how Frederick visualizes. Think about how it helps Frederick and his friends to visualize when the cold winter comes.

[Read *Frederick* aloud from start to finish without stopping. When you reach the last page, just close the book and sit quietly for a few seconds.]

Readers, Frederick showed his friends how visualizing could help them remember the good parts of spring and summer, even when the cold winter came. That's what we did. We visualized fun times on the playground, and that helps us hold on to those happy memories. Tomorrow we are going to explore how visualizing can help us make meaning when we read.

⊡ LESSON FOCUS Exploring Opportunities to Visualize as Readers

Readers, yesterday we read *Frederick* by Leo Lionni and explored how visualizing helped Frederick and his friends remember the good parts of spring and summer when they couldn't go out during the cold winter days. We could see all the memories they shared because Leo Lionni showed them in the illustrations. When a book has no illustrations we have to be like Frederick and his friends: We have to visualize the illustrations in our minds. Visualizing helps us make meaning.

Today I have two books, and I am going to read only a small part from each of them. I'd like you to close your eyes and visualize the illustrations as I read each part. We will read the entire book another day and enjoy the whole story and all the art.

[Have the lines you plan to read written in your notebook or typed on a page.]

The first reading comes from *Winter Is Coming* by Tony Johnston.

[Read the lines with a little drama to highlight the descriptive language.]

"It was a cold September day. Fall is still here but ice is in the air. I feel it. Winter is coming."

Readers, sit with those words for a few seconds and make an illustration in your mind.

[Pause as they visualize images and feelings.]

Share what you were seeing and feeling with your partner.

[Pause briefly. Then invite a few to share images and feelings evoked by the language.]

Let's try another. The next reading comes from *Billywise* by Judith Nicholls.

[Read the lines slowly with a little drama to highlight the descriptive language.]

"From the mole-black hole in the oldest oak, deep in the heart of the fern-brushed wood . . . a scritch, a scratch, a tap, a crack! A pale egg split . . ."

[Repeat the steps above.]

Let's try visualizing another way. I'll read a poem written by Judith Viorst. Your task is to listen and visualize. Then I'll ask you to sketch what your mind is seeing.

[Have the paper ready to distribute when you send them back to their seats to sketch.]

The poem is titled "Stanley the Fierce." Close your eyes and listen and visualize.

[Read the poem with a bit of drama that evokes the character.]

Let's sit with this poem for a moment. Notice the details in what you are visualizing.

[Pause briefly.]

Open your eyes and tell your partner what you noticed.

Readers, it sounds as if you have some interesting images in your mind. Let's hear from a few of you.

[Allow three or four students to offer some specific details.]

Now, as the paper comes around, take a sheet and return to your tables. When you are seated I'll read "Stanley the Fierce" one more time.

[Send them to their seats with paper and supplies.]

As I read this time listen closely for anything you may have missed. Think like Frederick, and see those images in your mind again. When I finish I'll ask you to make the illustration you are visualizing.

[Read the poem slowly and dramatically. Allow a few minutes for them to sketch.]

Let's pause here. Take a moment to share your sketches at your table. [We've included examples of student responses in Figures 9.1a, 9.1b, and 9.1c.] Talk about what your sketches have in common and how they are different.

[Pause briefly as they share.]

I'm noticing that most of you have drawn Stanley with big muscles and spiky hair. I saw a few that show Stanley's chipped tooth. I think everyone made Stanley's hands clenched in fists so we can't see his fingers. Some of you made Stanley's mouth very small with no smile. I also noticed his eyes. Judith Viorst tells us that his eyes give a shivery glare. Some of you made his eyes big and wide open, and some of you made little tiny dot eyes like he is squinting.

Readers, isn't it interesting that when we visualize we see some things just the way our friends see them. And other things are not at all the way our friends see them. Today as we move into our reading, let's try thinking like Frederick. Let's visualize and notice what we see in our minds as we read.

Figure 9.1a Stanley the Fierce—Evelyn, age 3

Figure 9.1b Stanley the Fierce—Ainsley, First Grade

Figure 9.1c Stanley the Fierce—Trent, Sixth Grade

Flip It from Reading to Writing

Visualizing is not just for readers. Writers also visualize. Writers often hold an image of a character in mind as they write. They have a vision of the setting and imagine their characters moving through time and spaces. Those visions may be constructed from a thousand moments in a thousand books or from a childhood memory or from an old house they saw in a painting while on vacation. But there is a vision. Some writers sketch a floor plan or an image of the locale to ground them in place. Images and sensory details waft through the minds of writers as they create texts. In fact, visualizing may be too limiting. What we do as readers and writers is broader than simply creating a visual image in our minds. We draw upon sensory memories as we generate verbal descriptions of what we have seen and felt and heard and tasted and smelled. We do our best to evoke in our readers a similar experience.

◧ LESSON FOCUS Exploring Opportunities to Visualize as Writers

Writers, we've been working on visualizing in reading. Today we are going to explore how visualizing can be a useful tool in our writing as well. Just like Frederick in Leo Lionni's book, I try to recall the images I have stored away before I write. Sometimes I make a sketch, and sometimes I can see it so clearly I am able to describe it with my words.

Yesterday we searched through our notebooks to find a topic for our personal narratives. I decided to write about a birthday party. First I'll just think about how that looks and try to remember all the fun things that happen.

[Pause briefly as you think.]

OK, I'm going to sketch what I remember on sticky notes. [See Figure 9.2a.]

[Pause, then talk about your thoughts and sketch four to six scenes and post them on the chart as you finish each one.]

Writers, visualizing helps me get organized. These sketches will help me remember the important details.

After I sketch, I write a note on each one to help me remember what I will write about on each page. [See Figure 9.2b.] Now I'm ready to start my draft.

I will look at each sketch and the note I wrote when I begin to draft each scene in my story.

Writers, yesterday you chose a topic from your notebooks. Today when you are in your writing spot, I'd like you to take a few moments to think about your topic and visualize what you'd like to write about. Try starting with a few sketches on these sticky notes to capture those ideas. Then jot a note that will help you remember what you will write about on each page. Let's get started.

Figure 9.2a Post-it Sketches

My mom made my favorite cake.

I made a wish and blew out the candles.

Everyone sang happy birthday and we ate cake.

I got lots of presents.

It was a very happy day!

Figure 9.2b Post-it Sketches with Notes

Writing Samples

Francisco used his reader insights to visualize and record his thoughts in a sketch. That helped him maintain focus as he wrote a summary of the important ideas he wants to include in his draft (see Figure 9.3).

Allen visualized to recall a recent visit to Sea World. His sketch allows him to capture those thoughts as a placeholder while he is developing the vocabulary to express his ideas more fully (see Figure 9.4).

Figure 9.3 Francisco, First Grade
(ELL student)

Figure 9.4 Allen, First Grade
(ELL student)

Additional Texts: Visualizing

Birds by Kevin Henkes: This book asks the reader to imagine what the sky would look like if birds of all colors made marks with their feathers as they flew. What would those marks look like? If the clouds were birds, what would they look like? The brief text invites visualization.

The Emperor's Egg by Martin Jenkins: This informational text explains how the father penguin keeps the egg warm while the mother goes in search of food. Although the illustrations are lovely, the language is richly descriptive and will evoke images in the minds of listeners and readers.

The Iridescence of Birds: A Book About Henri Matisse by Patricia MacLachlan: Rich and vivid language describing the formative years of Henri Matisse's life will ignite visual images in the reader's mind.

"Lost and Finds" by Rebecca Kai Dotlich (in *Falling Down the Page*, edited by Georgia Heard): This poem is a treasure trove of items familiar to young readers. There are many opportunities for visualizing.

10

NOTICING
IMPORTANT DETAILS

Very young children are constantly encouraged to notice and name things in the world around them. Imagine a toddler stepping through a garden, one of his arms reaching up and his small hand wrapped around a grandfather's index finger. Along the way the grandfather stops, bends down beside the child, and points to something, perhaps a butterfly, and says, "Look. There's a butterfly. Do you see the butterfly?" The toddler reaches in the direction of the delicate creature and utters his best version of "butterfly." The idea of noticing the unusual, the beautiful, the out of the ordinary, the unexpected, is something we cultivate across a life. The garden is full of beauty, but the significant noticing today is the presence of a butterfly. From that experience the toddler will notice other butterflies and likely delight in naming each one: "Butterfly." In future visits to the garden the child will scan the flower blossoms looking for the butterfly, and when he spies one he will point and call his grandfather's attention to the beauty of this creature. The grandfather will confirm the sighting and delight in the child's noticing. More important, the child becomes a "noticer," one who is tuned in to what is going on around him.

All through our lives we learn to attend to our surroundings, to note those things that may signal danger or opportunity. We note the unusual, the extraordinary, the beautiful, the frightening. We note the exhilarating, the challenging, the horrific, the threatening. We note what falls outside our "normal." The fact that we notice does not make anything significant or important. It merely means that it was outside our expectation, beyond the scope of our typical experience. It is that "difference" that captures our attention. The significance, if any, is determined by the meaning we make of it. Significance is assigned when the noticing makes a difference in our understanding, when it has an effect on our actions or decisions. If that effect is powerful enough we learn to assign greater significance and are more likely to notice similar things with less effort in the future.

Our students have life experience with noticing and assigning significance to events in their lives. They have experience with deciding whether something is worth their attention. If we can tap that experience and sharpen their focus, we can more easily help them make meaning from their engagements with texts.

✦ LESSON FOCUS Introduce the Concept of Noticing Important Details

Readers, every day we wash our hands and line up and walk down the hall to the lunchroom. Every day we follow the same routine. Every day as we pass the kindergarten classrooms, they are always sitting in a circle listening to a story as we pass by. We expect those kids to be sitting in a circle on the rug listening to a story. So now we almost don't notice because, well, it's the ordinary thing that happens . . . every day.

When things become ordinary we may not even think about them anymore. We don't even think about what is happening in the lunchroom because the same thing happens every day. We walk in, move through the serving lines, get our lunches, take a seat at our table, and eat lunch. Ordinary. Ordinary. Ordinary.

But what if something important was planned for next Friday, and the principal wanted all the third graders to be in the lunchroom at 1:00 p.m.? What could she do to spotlight that information and make sure we know about it? Think for a few seconds, then talk with your neighbor about three things our principal could do to spotlight the information so we know it is important for us to be there.

[Pause a few seconds for the brainstorming.]

Let me hear a few of your thoughts.

- ✦ Posters in the hall
- ✦ A big message on the bulletin board outside the lunchroom door
- ✦ An announcement on the morning news

Readers, if our principal put a big message for third graders on the bulletin board outside the lunchroom, we would notice. It would get our attention because it would be unusual and because it is about us.

Often when information is important, writers will make it noticeable. That is kind of like putting a spotlight on the idea. They may use bright colors or big letters or bold print or italics to get our attention. Writers may add extra details or use dialog to get our attention and make us notice. Readers, we notice when something is out of the ordinary. And then we have to decide whether it is important. Over the next few days we will be exploring how writers work to spotlight ideas to help us notice what is important.

➡ LESSON FOCUS Exploring Opportunities for Noticing Important Details as Readers of Fiction

Readers, we have been exploring how writers help us notice what is important. Today we are going to revisit one part of a best friend book, *Jamaica's Find* by Juanita Havill. [Open the book to the spread where Jamaica is lying on the grass holding the red hat and looking at the stuffed dog.]

In this part of the story Jamaica finds a hat and a stuffed dog. Juanita Havill puts a spotlight on the stuffed dog in this scene. I'll read this page. Notice how Juanita lets us know the dog is going to be more important than the hat.

[Read the page slowly. Let your voice draw attention to the specific details provided about the dog.]

Of course we know the dog is very important in the story because we have visited this book many times. This time think about what Juanita Havill did that let us know the dog was so important.

[Pause briefly.]

Readers, share your thoughts with your partner.

[Pause briefly.]

I heard most of you noticing all the details Juanita gave us about the dog. Yet, she didn't tell us much at all about the hat. For example, we know the hat is red and it is a sock hat. That's all, just two things. But we know the dog is stuffed and cuddly and gray, it is worn and stained, and it has a missing nose and two black ears.

Readers, Juanita Havill put a spotlight on the dog with details that zoom in to help us notice. Since she gives us zoom-in details only about the dog, we expect the dog to be important in this story. Using details that zoom in is one way a writer can spotlight an important idea.

I'll begin a chart where we can keep track of the different ways a writer can spotlight important information for us.

Today as we move out to read, if you notice that the author spotlights something with zoom in details mark it with a sticky note. Then read on and find out if that was a signal for something important in the story.

◆ LESSON FOCUS Exploring Opportunities for Noticing Important Details as Readers of Nonfiction

Readers, we are going to continue exploring how writers spotlight important information to help us make meaning. Today we are going to revisit one part of *Hope for Winter: The True Story of a Remarkable Dolphin Friendship* by Craig Hatkoff and David Yates.

We read this book a few times during our study of mammals, but today we are going to think about how these writers spotlight significant details that help us make meaning.

Let's begin with the cover. When we read this book for science, we noticed a title and a subtitle, *Hope for Winter: The True Story of a Remarkable Dolphin Friendship*.

Remember how we predicted this would be a nonfiction book because the subtitle says the *true* story?

Talk with your partner, and decide whether this is a spotlight on important ideas.

[Pause very briefly.]

Thumbs up for yes, thumbs down for no.

Wow, everyone says yes, this is a spotlight. So that one word, *true*, is like a spotlight that helps us notice this is a nonfiction book. Knowing that a book is nonfiction gets our thinking ready for facts and information.

Let's look for another spotlight. The authors wrote a letter to the readers. I'll read it, and you decide whether the letter could be a spotlight on important ideas. It begins, "To Our Readers . . ."

[Read the letter aloud.]

Talk with your partner and decide whether this letter is a spotlight for readers. Be ready to offer a reason for your decision.

[Allow time to share thinking and negotiation.]

Thumbs up for yes, thumbs down for no.

We are all in agreement that the letter spotlights important information. I noticed these facts:

- ♦ Hope and Winter are two dolphins.

- ♦ Both dolphins were rescued by the aquarium.

- ♦ Winter was injured and lost her tail.

- ♦ Winter had to learn to swim again.

- ♦ Winter lost her partner, a dolphin named Panama.

- ♦ Dolphins are very social animals and need a partner to be stable.

- ♦ Hope was found abandoned, and the people from the aquarium rescued her.

- ♦ The rescue team was hoping that Hope and Winter would become friends.

Readers, these facts focus our thinking and help us know what to expect as we read.

Let's look for another spotlight. The next page is a photograph with a caption. This book has several photographs, and each photograph has a caption.

[Turn several pages showing the photographs and captions.]

I'm going to turn each page slowly and read only the captions for each photograph. Listen carefully and you'll notice something interesting.

[Present the first photograph, read the caption, and continue to the end.]

Did you notice when we view the photographs and read the captions we make a kind of summary of the book? So, these photographs and captions are another kind of spotlight for us. These help us get an image in our minds as we read, and they remind us of the sequence of the important details in *this* book.

I'll add these ways to spotlight information to our chart.

Today as you move out to read, tune in to the ways the author spotlights important information in your text. If you notice anything we haven't added to our chart, flag it with a sticky note and bring it to our reading workshop tomorrow. Let's talk about what writers do that helps us make meaning.

Flip It from Reading to Writing

Writers begin with a focus and a sense of what is important. Readers look for spotlights and signals for what is important, but writers select what to spotlight and how to do it. Writers layer in specific details and make use of author notes and employ the text features such as headings and bold print and charts and captions. Writers work to help readers make sense.

⊟ LESSON FOCUS Exploring Opportunities for Noticing Important Details as Writers

Writers, we have been exploring how to decide what is important when we read. We discovered that writers often spotlight important ideas to help us. If we want to do this for our readers, there are two things we have to do.

First, we have to decide which ideas are the most important for our readers to know. Second, we have to choose how we are going to spotlight those ideas. Let's take a look at the chart we made as readers. I think we can use some of these items to spotlight our most important ideas to help our readers know what we think is most important.

[Review the chart.]

I've shown you some of the entries in my notebook for my honeybee project, and you've helped me make some

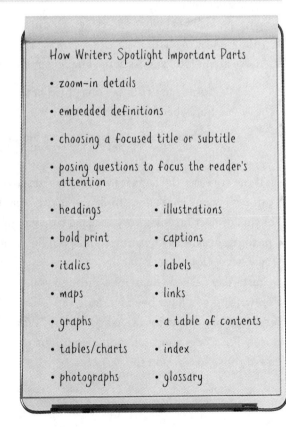

How Writers Spotlight Important Parts

- zoom-in details

- embedded definitions

- choosing a focused title or subtitle

- posing questions to focus the reader's attention

- headings
- bold print
- italics
- maps
- graphs
- tables/charts
- photographs

- illustrations
- captions
- labels
- links
- a table of contents
- index
- glossary

decisions about my work. Today I am going to return to the fact list and the planning summary I wrote with you when I was getting my thoughts organized.

Remember, my plan is to write a nonfiction text that will let readers know how important honeybees are in the world. Take a look at these.

[Show the list and summary page from the notebook—see page 75.]

Now that I'm thinking about ways to spotlight what is most important, I must be very focused. If I spotlight everything or too many things, my readers will be confused. So I'm going to start with what I really want my readers to know.

There are several interesting facts on my list, like the different kinds of bees and that all the worker bees are females and how bees make honey. But, my focus is to let the reader know how important bees are to the world. So take a moment to read my list and planning summary again. Help me decide which ideas I should spotlight.

[Pause briefly.]

Share your thinking with your partner.

[Pause briefly.]

Writers, let's hear what you've agreed on.

[Allow a few to share.]

Those are helpful suggestions. I believe most of us are in agreement on these two:

- Some scientists say one-third of all the crops in the world depend on honeybees for pollination.
- If there were no honeybees we wouldn't have as many fruits, vegetables, and nuts to eat.

These are essential facts if I want my reader to know why honeybees are important. Now I can review our chart and think about the best way to spotlight these ideas in my draft. For this project I think a very focused title will be helpful. And I think perhaps I could use a heading. Maybe my heading could even be a question. Writers, thank you for your help. Now I have a lot of work to do.

Yesterday I asked you to look through your writing folders and choose a piece of nonfiction writing you have been working on. Today I'd like you to reread that piece and think carefully about your focus. Ask yourself, "What do I really want readers to know?" Look closely for places you could add a spotlight that would be helpful to your reader. Choose two of those to work on today.

Writing Samples

In these two samples Alex draws upon his reader insights about signaling significant details and layers in illustrations and captions (see Figure 10.1).

Figure 10.1 Alex, First Grade

All About

Comparasons

big , bigger, biggest!
small, smaller, smallest!
thick, thiker, thickest!
fast faster fastest!
loud louder loudest
Wide more Wide Widest

The goose fly The highest.

The chicken flys higher

The penguin flys the lowest. It dosn't even fly!

Additional Texts: Noticing Important Details

Birmingham, 1963 by Carole Boston Weatherford: This story recounts the tragic events of September 15 at the Sixteenth Street Baptist Church in Birmingham, Alabama, when a bomb killed four young girls. Each page of the brief book is paired with black-and-white photographs from the era, and the story is laced with factual information revealing the dangers of the time. There are ample opportunities to read with an eye for noticing significant detail.

The Bobbin Girl by Emily Arnold McCully: This book is set in the early 1800s and is based on a true story of poor working conditions faced by young girls employed in a mill. In this time young girls worked to help their families survive. When the owners cut wages, workers were forced to decide whether to stand up for their rights with the risk of getting fired. The story is rich with detail about working conditions, living conditions in the boarding house, and the desperate need for children to make money. Readers have ample opportunity to consider what is important as they weave an understanding of life for girls in the 1800s.

The Great Kapok Tree by Lynne Cherry: This book takes readers into the rain forest and describes how each element of plant life provides essential habitat to various species of animals. Readers will explore the importance of plant life and come to appreciate the interdependence of flora and fauna in the rain forest. When men begin to cut down trees, an imbalance occurs that affects life in the forest. Because of this interdependency readers get to determine what facts are essential for the rain forest to remain healthy and survive, which in turn affects each of the animals and their survival.

Locomotive by Brian Floca: This picture book gives the history of building railroads across America. The book offers a wealth of information about various elements of the locomotive. Readers will want to approach this book with focus and purpose. The text could be read and revisited several times, returning with a different focus for each reading (e.g., geography within the story, how people became dependent on the ease of transportation afforded by the locomotive, and so on).

11

MAKING
CONNECTIONS

Connections just happen. Sometimes it seems that the brain is a connection magnet. Driving down the street you pass a group of kids playing freeze tag on the lawn of a neighbor's home and—*poof*—your brain pings back in time. There you are, remembering a moment from your past. Step into a bakery and catch the smell of cinnamon and nutmeg—*poof*—in a flash you are recalling some holiday kitchen from your childhood. No, it doesn't take much to trigger those moments. We experience that unexpected flash without effort, without conscious thought. At times that flash of connection catches us off guard and sends us tracing threads of our lives deep into the tapestry. It may trigger a moment of deep reflection or a stream of tears. It may trigger uncontrollable giggles. It may be a shared experience or a solitary one. Connections just happen.

Connections pull up threads from our personal history (family, friends, holiday gatherings, celebrations, weddings, funerals, school days, shopping trips, vacations, and ordinary, mundane, almost-forgotten events). It is probably safe to assume that each of us has experienced those moments when an event triggers a connection to a scene from a movie, a line in a song, a poem, a story, or something from a favorite book. Every time I'm in a restaurant and hear someone having a great time, I have a flash from a now-iconic movie and think, "I'll have what she's having." And, if you've lived long enough to have a bit of history in the world, you'll find yourself watching the news and being reminded of events from our collective past, events from politics, human suffering, human celebration, war, and more. Connections just happen.

Of course, the now ubiquitous phrases (text-to-self, text-to-text, text-to-world) have convinced teachers of the power of connections in the reading lives of our students. Lester is frequently in schools as a visiting author or author-in-residence and can attest to the almost involuntary text-to-self connections that erupt from children during and following a shared story. Connections just happen.

There is power in these connections. Connections remind us that we are not in this world alone. They remind us that literature and art and media have the power to link us to our past, to one another, to others we have met, and to those we may never meet. Connections help us to recognize that our background knowledge and schema can be powerful tools for making sense of new experiences whether firsthand or vicariously in some text or another.

Consciously tapping those connections as readers can help us understand situations, can give us the ability to have empathy with characters, can enable us to infer and predict, and can assist us in making decisions about the veracity of content. Connections just happen, but becoming conscious of them and harnessing the power of them takes time and instruction.

◧ LESSON FOCUS   Introduce the Concept of Connecting

[Note: You will need paper towels, rubber bands, sealable plastic sandwich bags, and ground coffee. Place a teaspoon of ground coffee in a paper towel, pull the corners up, and twist and seal with a rubber band. Put one of these in a plastic sandwich bag and seal it. You'll need six to eight of these.]

Readers, our brains make connections all the time. It's almost like you can't stop it. Today we are going to explore how our brains connect to what we have experienced and how that helps us make sense of what is going on around us.

I have several sandwich bags with me today in this tub. In a moment I'll send these bags around and ask you to open them. You will not need to hold the bag. You'll smell it. The second you open them you will know what is inside, just from the smell, but do not say anything. Remember, do not say anything.

Instead I want you to sit and think about what this smell makes you think of. Think about what you see in your mind. What sounds does it make you remember? Is there a person this smell makes you think of? Or maybe a place this smell pulls up in your thoughts. Just sit with the smell and your thoughts. Remember, do not say anything.

[Hand out the bags. When they are all distributed ask the students to open them at the same time.]

Readers, sit with this smell and let your brain make connections. Just close your eyes and be aware of what you start remembering.

[Pause briefly.]

Turn to your partner and share some of the images and sounds and memories that popped up in your brain.

[Pause briefly.]

Let's hear a few of those connections.

[As they share, stop and ask how many others had a similar image or memory. Some images and sensory memories will be unique to the individual, but some will be common to the group.]

Readers, connections just happen. They happen every day. Connections can be triggered by a smell like the coffee we just sniffed. Connections can be triggered by something we see or hear or even by things we read. Connections just happen.

Over the next few days we will begin exploring how connections can help us make meaning when we read and when we write.

⊡ LESSON FOCUS Exploring Opportunities to Make Connections as Readers

Readers, we've been exploring how our connections with texts help us make meaning more personal and relevant. Connections help us use what we know from our experiences, from other texts, or from something going on in the world to understand what the writer is presenting on the page. Connections move our thinking beyond the page.

For our first read-aloud this morning I read *Those Shoes* by Maribeth Boelts. I told you then we would come back to it during reading workshop.

I'll read a page or two and pause for you to think about the connections that are happening in your mind. We can say the connection in one or two sentences, but for this lesson I want you to focus on what is happening in the writing or the art that triggers your connection. Think about how the writer helped you to think beyond the page.

Let me show you what I mean.

[Read the title, show the cover, and read the first spread.]

When we read the cover and first page I remembered that when I was in school I wished for the expensive jeans that were in all the magazines. Some kids at school had them, and I didn't.

Two things happened in the book that made me think of that. One is in the art where the cool shoes are being advertised on the billboards and some kids are wearing them. The second thing is when the kid said he had dreams of those shoes.

Readers, making connections is the easy part. Today I want to push our thinking a bit more and notice what the writer does to trigger our connections. Let's give that a try.

[Read the next two spreads.]

Sit with these two pages in your mind. Think about the connections in your brain and then think about what the author and illustrator did that made that happen.

[Pause briefly.]

Talk with your partner about that.

[Pause briefly.]

Readers, I heard so many connections. Here are a few of them.

- ◆ "My mom says we have to get what we need, and then we can talk about what we want."

- ◆ "I saw a commercial that tries to make you believe you will lose weight if you drink their stuff."

- ◆ "I know this guy in fifth grade who tries to make everybody notice his new jacket."

- ◆ "In second grade most people came to school with new book bags, but me and a couple of other kids had the same ones from first grade, and I wished for a new book bag."

Now talk about what happened on these pages that tickled your brain and made you remember these things.

[Pause briefly.]

Readers, I'll return to these pages. Let's begin here. [Present the page with the grandma in the chair.] What did the author or illustrator do here that tickled your brain?

- ◆ "When the grandma says, there's no room for want around here . . . that made me remember what my mom says."

♦ "When I saw the buildings out the window and the treetops, it made me think of staying in a hotel in the city."

And what tickled your brain on this page? [Turn to the next page.]

♦ "When that kid said that boy went to the bathroom seven times just so people would see his shoes, it made me think about the guy I know in fifth grade."

♦ "And when that kid said he's the fastest now because he got those shoes, I thought of the commercial I saw once. He says that because the commercials try to make you believe it."

♦ "I thought about my first-grade book bag in second grade when I saw that kid standing in line for lunch, and he's the only one that didn't have those new shoes."

Since we read *Those Shoes* this morning for our first read-aloud, I'm going to skip over to another part of the story.

[Turn to the spread where Antonio comes over and sees "those shoes" in his bedroom. Read that spread and the next one.]

Readers, talk about your connections and what the author and illustrator did to help. [Pause briefly.]

Talk with me now. Tell me what the writer or illustrator did and how that helped you make a connection.

♦ "When Antonio asked about the shoes and the kid could feel him wishing for the shoes, I thought about my little cousin who comes to my house sometimes and plays with some of my old toys that I had when I was little like him."

♦ "When the kid got up early and ran over and left the shoes on Antonio's steps, I remembered that book (*The Teddy Bear* by David McPhail) you read to us about that little boy who forget his teddy bear and a homeless guy found it. Then the boy gave the teddy bear to the homeless man.

Let's take a moment now to name what the writer did to help us remember and make connections.

♦ Writers include details that most people will recognize, like the kid dreaming about getting those shoes or a grownup saying you can't get everything you want. Those are things that most of us thought about.

- Writers use language that sounds familiar. The way the grandmother talks may sound like something your parents or grandparents might say.

- Writers choose settings we can relate to, like the apartment he lived in, the stores where he went searching for those shoes, the school, the cafeteria, and the playground. When we read about those in a book we can imagine the places we know.

- Writers choose situations we understand like wanting something that is popular, not having enough money to get what you want, and feeling disappointed when others have something you are wishing for.

Readers, there are two things I would like you to continue thinking about as you go out to read in the room this morning.

- First, notice that when we read we seem to make connections automatically. It's almost like we don't even have to try. Connections help us understand what the character is feeling or thinking because we have thought or felt something like that ourselves. Connections also help us think about things around us, things in the world that aren't in the book, and that can help us think about ideas in a new way.

- Second, when you make a connection, pause and think about what the writer did to help you make that happen.

Flip It from Reading to Writing

Connections serve writers. Connections link writers to the stories of their own lives, stories they may have forgotten. Connections help writers tap into the universal themes of humanity. Connections help writers gain perspective and tap their passions and interests. Connections are a frequent source of information in the work of writers. When writers tap into those connections they weave a fiber through the fabric of the text that will reach into the lives of many, and that makes for more engaged readers. Typically our instruction in reading has a focus on the act of making the connections and using the relationship to heighten our understanding as readers. But to flip that thinking into informed opportunities for writers, we have to help the reader recognize what triggered the connection and name how it happened. Then the writer can weave those fibers into the fabric of their own work.

W riters, we have been exploring how connections with the text can help us make sense of what we are reading. Today we are going to flip that idea over and think about how our connections can help us when we write.

Turn to a clean page in your notebook, put your pencil in, and close it, please.

I am going to read two small stories from this collection. It is called, *In My Momma's Kitchen* by Jerdine Nolen. [Hold the book so the cover is visible.]

I know that your brain will be making all sorts of connections as I read to you, so get ready. The first story is called "Great-Aunt Caroline." There are only two illustrations so let's take a look at those first. This woman is Great-Aunt Caroline. She has a walking stick. She is ninety-five years old. The young girl in this illustration is our narrator.

[Turn the page.] On this page we see Great-Aunt Caroline and the girl going for a walk.

Writers, I know your brains are already making connections. Perhaps you're thinking about someone you know who has white hair like Great-Aunt Caroline. Or maybe you're thinking about someone who is very old or a person who uses a walking stick.

When connections remind you of something or someone you know, that could be a story tickling your writing brain.

Writers, if your brain begins making connections while I'm reading, just open your notebook and jot them down. Your pencil and a clean page are waiting for those connections.

[Read at a slow but deliberate pace with expression that highlights the mood. When you reach the end, sit quietly for about 20 seconds.]

Writers, let me stop you for a moment. I'm going to read this once more. This time I'll stop in a few places and nudge your thinking a bit. Get your pencil and notebook ready. As I talk us through this, jot down any connections you are making.

[Read the first four paragraphs.]

She is ninety-five. Think about anyone you know who is very old.

When she comes to visit, everyone has to be so quiet. Do you have to be very quiet around anyone? Was there a time when you were told to go outside to play?

Remember, if connections are happening in your brain, write down just enough to make you remember.

Do you know anyone who doesn't like to be around cats or dogs or pets? Hmmmm, maybe there is a story there.

Is there someone who comes to visit and isn't used to children, so you and your friends have to play outside? Is there a story there?

[Read to the end.]

She named her walking stick Henry. Perhaps you know someone who names things that aren't people or pets?

[Pause briefly while the pencils are moving.]

Writers, you are getting a lot of ideas on those pages. Write until your brain runs out.

[Turn to another vignette in the collection, and repeat these steps.]

Writers, rest your pencil on the page where you were writing and close the notebook. Now you have a long list of options to choose from when you are ready to start a new piece. From now on when I read aloud I'd like you to have your writer's notebook out and ready just in case you have connections that could become a story.

[Note: As students begin to lift connections from their notebooks to create stories or characters or scenes, remind them to think about what other writers did to help them make connections. Writing with that in mind helps the writer also connect with her audience.]

Writing Samples

Anthony makes note of personal connections during read-aloud experiences. Note that his draft of *It's Mine* grew out of an entry triggered by a personal connection when listening to a selection from *In My Momma's Kitchen* by Jerdine Nolen (see Figure 11.1).

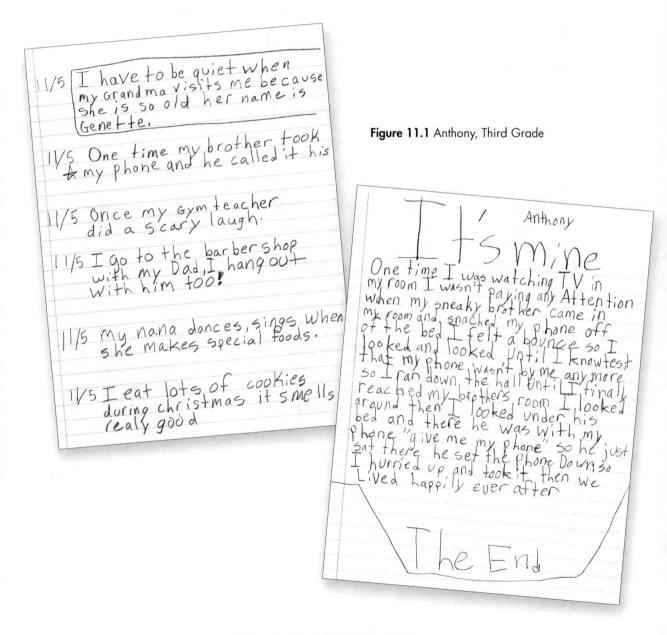

Figure 11.1 Anthony, Third Grade

11/5 I have to be quiet when my grandma visits me because she is so old her name is Genette.

11/5 One time my brother took my phone and he called it his

11/5 Once my gym teacher did a scary laugh.

11/5 I go to the barber shop with my Dad, I hang out with him too!

11/5 My nana dances, sings when she makes special foods.

11/5 I eat lots of cookies during christmas it smells really good

It's mine
Anthony

One time I was watching TV in my room I wasn't paying any Attention when my sneaky brother came in my room and snached my phone off of the bed I felt a bounce so I looked and looked until I knowtest that my phone wasn't by me anymore so I ran down the hall until I finally reached my brothers room I looked around then I looked under his bed and there he was with my phone "give me my phone" so he just sat there he set the phone down so I hurried up and took it then we lived happily ever after

The End

Additional Texts: Making Connections

Alexander and the Terrible, Horrible, No Good, Very Bad Day by Judith Viorst: Almost every reader can make a connection with Alexander. After all, haven't we all had mornings where nothing goes as planned? Alexander's bad day began the minute he stepped foot out of bed and continued all day. Because most children can relate to his mishaps, this would be a good text to begin your study on making connections.

The Matchbox Diary by Paul Fleischman: This book is filled with possibilities for making connections as the great-grandfather shares with his great-granddaughter the memories he has stored in tiny matchboxes across his long life. This story presents several opportunities for connections with a family member, an older friend, an interest in collecting something, or recording your memories.

The Soccer Fence: A True Story of Friendship, Hope, and Apartheid in South Africa by Phil Bildner: This picture book is filled with possibilities for making connections: world events, relationships, hopes, dreams, and the love of the game of soccer. Hector lived in South Africa and loved the game of soccer, but because his nation was so restrictive he lived a very isolated life. He dreamed of playing on a real field with other boys. When Nelson Mandela was freed from prison, apartheid ended. Slowly things changed, and one day Hector was invited to play soccer on a real field.

What If . . . ? by Anthony Browne: This book highlights many of the questions and doubts a young boy and his mother have about Joe going to a party in a strange neighborhood. Most of the attention of the story goes to the boy's doubts. But when the mother turns to walk away, leaving her son at the party, her doubts surface.

SECTION 3

STORY ELEMENTS

As teachers we know story. We know about characters and setting and plot. We know about story arcs and the all-important beginning-middle-end. We know about perspective and point of view. As teachers we know about rising action and exposition and tension. We know about climax and conclusion. Story is something we know.

As teachers we get excited about reading aloud to our students and sharing story with them. But we need to remind ourselves that some of our students have never snuggled into a cozy chair with a dad and an opened picture book. Some of them have not heard a story read aloud. They do not know that words on the page give voice to characters in the art. Some of our students have never heard anyone tell of Goldilocks and the Three Bears, or The Three Little Pigs, or Little Red Riding Hood. They will not know that the phrase "once upon a time . . ." is the front door to a folktale. Some of our students will come to us having never heard of "a land far away" or "an enchanted forest" or "a little cottage in the woods." They will not know the power of place in the flow of story. There are students who have yet to meet a character so engaging she finds her way into their play and into their dreams without effort.

As teachers we cannot assume anything. We begin with story, and we visit and revisit and visit again as we build students' understanding of the elements present in all stories. As teachers we introduce our students to a host of characters and help them navigate through an array of settings—both physical and emotional. As they move through story with new on-the-page friends, wishing their wishes and dreaming their dreams, we stand at the ready if they need us.

The story elements that seem so commonplace to us may be anything but common to our students. In this section we explore character, setting, and plot (including conflict/tension/resolution) and add a bit on perspective and point of view.

12

CHARACTER

E ven as children we come to know particular characters in our lives. There's the uncle who makes the best cheesecake, the cousin who makes everyone crack up with that puppet, and the neighbor who sits on the front porch with fourteen cats swarming around. We all have characters in our lives. And they are often surrounded by story. Sometimes we hear about them and have a sense of knowing them, even if we never meet them in person. We may pass them every day and say nothing more than "good morning." We come to know the characters in our lives layer by layer. But those characters, all of them, play a role in the story of who we are.

⏩ LESSON FOCUS Exploring Character as Readers

R eaders, we've read *The Snowy Day* and *Whistle for Willie* and *Peter's Chair*, three books by Ezra Jack Keats in which Peter is the main character. We've thought a lot about Peter and looked for evidence that helps us know who Peter is and what he is like.

We thought about how we would finish this sentence: Peter is the kind of boy who . . .

We came up with several ideas and decided that Peter is a bit mischievous and that he likes playing jokes on people.

Today, we are going to revisit *Peter's Chair*. We already know what happens and what Peter did. This time I want you to focus your thinking on what Ezra Jack Keats does to help us know about Peter.

I'll read the first two pages and show you what I mean.

[Read the first two spreads.]

I believe Peter is a boy who is careful and works hard.

Ezra Jack Keats helps me know that when he says Peter reached as high as he could to finish his tall building. And the art shows Peter being very careful to place the last block on the tower.

And I believe that Peter is a boy who doesn't get angry often. Ezra helped me think that when he shows Willie running through and crashing the tower, but Peter doesn't get angry.

So at this point I would say:

◆ Peter is the kind of boy who is careful and works hard and doesn't get angry much.

◆ Ezra tells us and shows us how Peter worked on a project.

◆ Ezra shows us how Peter reacts when things go wrong.

As I read the next few pages I'd like you to notice what Ezra Jack Keats does to help us know more about Peter.

[Read the next four spreads, stopping with the one where Peter picks up the chair.]

Readers, sit with these ideas, and think about how Ezra Jack Keats is letting us know more about Peter. Get your thoughts ready, "Peter is the kind of boy who . . . and Ezra helped me believe that when he . . ."

[Pause briefly.]

Share your thinking with your partner.

[Pause briefly.]

What have you noticed?

◆ Peter is a boy who can get his feelings hurt and feel jealous.

◆ Ezra let us hear what Peter was thinking in his head.

◆ Ezra let us hear what Peter whispers and mutters when his parents didn't hear.

◆ Ezra lets us see what Peter was doing when parents didn't see.

I think you've got it. I'll read to the end of the book, and your job is to focus on what we learn about Peter and how Ezra Jack Keats helps us to notice.

[Read to the end of the book and repeat the process above.]

What have you noticed?

◆ Peter is a boy who likes to play jokes. He is mischievous.

◆ Ezra tells us what Peter is thinking.

◆ Ezra shows us what the mom sees so we can know what she is thinking about Peter.

- Ezra lets us see Peter play the joke on his mom.

- Peter is a boy who can change his mind.

- Ezra tells us the chair is too little.

- Ezra let us see Peter try out the chair.

- Ezra let us hear Peter suggest they paint the chair pink for sister.

Readers, let's summarize what we have discovered today about how we come to know a character. [Jot these comments in your notebook and make a chart for later reference.] We learn about characters when

- we read what characters are thinking.

- we read what characters are saying.

- we read what characters are doing.

- the narrator tells us about them.

- we read how the character reacts to events.

Today as you move out to read, pause along the way and think about what you are coming to know about your character. You may even say in your brain, "So far I'm thinking this character is the kind of person who . . ." Pause now and then and think about what is on the page that helped you.

Flip It from Reading to Writing

Knowing the character is essential to writing story. The writer has to understand the character well enough to know how she will act and react to situations, what her response will be, how her voice sounds, and ten things she would never do. The writer has to understand what motivates a character and what she is passionate about, how she chooses friends, and whether she likes jellybeans or green beans or no beans at all. The more a writer knows about the character, the more a reader will come to believe in that character. So as we read and meet characters we love (and perhaps a few we just don't like), we must also look closely with a writer's lens and find out how the writer made that happen. The insights we develop as attuned readers will lead us to informed writing.

⬏ LESSON FOCUS Exploring Character as Writers

Writers, we have been thinking about how our reading can inform our writing. In our reading work we have been exploring how writers help us come to know the characters in a story. Today we are going to begin thinking about how we can use those insights to help our readers discover what we want them to know about our characters.

Let's begin with a look at the chart we have been building in our reading work.

We can help our readers discover our characters when we

- ⬍ let them hear what the character is thinking.

- ⬍ let them hear what the character is saying.

- ⬍ let them see what the character is doing (even if the other characters don't see it).

- ⬍ use the narrator's voice to tell about the character.

- ⬍ let them see how the character reacts to events.

Writers, one way we can get our thoughts organized before beginning a draft is to jot our thoughts about the main character. I've been thinking about writing a story about a pig that doesn't like to do anything the other pigs do. So to help me get my ideas organized, I gave my pig a name, William Walter Wallowsworth. I wrote his name at the top of a page in my notebook. Then I began to think about what I would like my readers to know about him, and I made this list. Let's take a look.

[Show the notebook pages, Figure 12.1.]

This list gives me something to think about as I'm getting my ideas together for the story. Now that I know what William likes and doesn't like and what he thinks about and wishes for and worries about, I can begin to imagine some of the problems he would face while living on a farm in Virginia. As I think about that I'll most likely add or change a few things on this list.

Writers, let's try this out. Think about the main character in the story you are working on right now. Open your notebook to a new page, and write that character's name at the top.

Now pause a moment, and think about three things you would like your reader to know about that character.

You might say it this way, "When my reader finishes the story I want him to say that character is the kind of person who . . ."

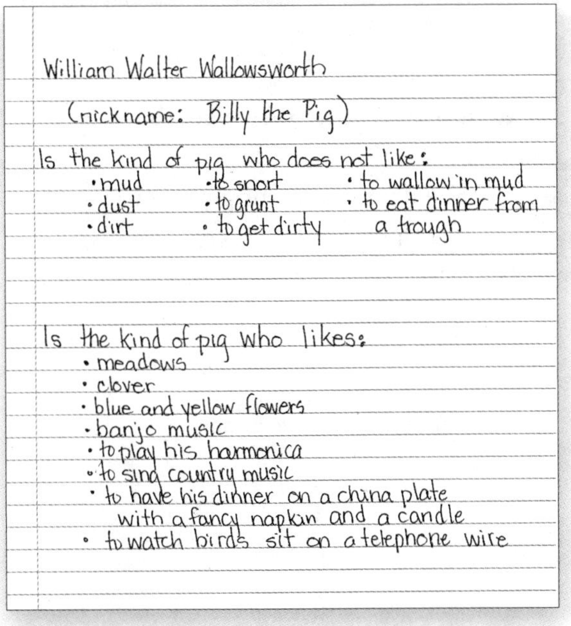

William Walter Wallowsworth

(nickname: Billy the Pig)

Is the kind of pig who does not like:
- mud
- dust
- dirt
- to snort
- to grunt
- to get dirty
- to wallow in mud
- to eat dinner from a trough

Is the kind of pig who likes:
- meadows
- clover
- blue and yellow flowers
- banjo music
- to play his harmonica
- to sing country music
- to have his dinner on a china plate with a fancy napkin and a candle
- to watch birds sit on a telephone wire

Figure 12.1 William Walter Wallowsworth

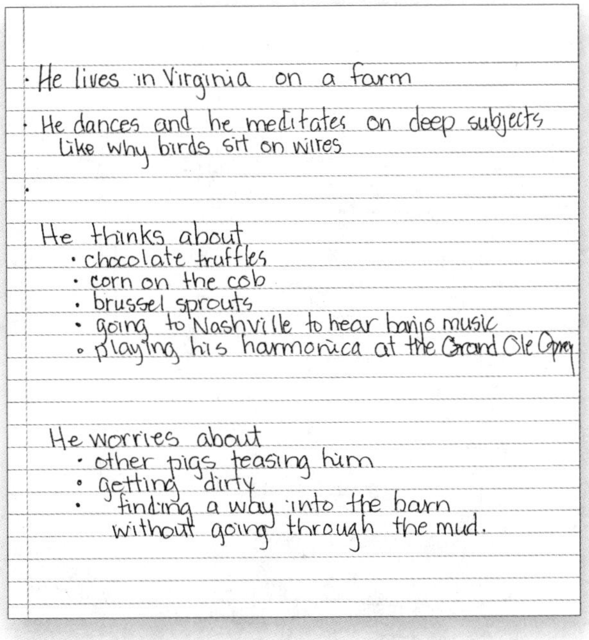

- He lives in Virginia on a farm
- He dances and he meditates on deep subjects like why birds sit on wires

He thinks about
- chocolate truffles
- corn on the cob
- brussel sprouts
- going to Nashville to hear banjo music
- playing his harmonica at the Grand Ole Opry

He worries about
- other pigs teasing him
- getting dirty
- finding a way into the barn without going through the mud.

Now jot those ideas in your notebook: _____ is the kind of person who . . .

[Pause briefly as they write.]

Writers, today as you move out to your writing spot I'd like you to try something. Sit with your notebook open to this page, and take a few more minutes to think about your main character. Jot down all the things you know about that character. You may write it in lists like I did in my notebook, or try it another way.

After that I'd like you to return to your draft and look for places where you are letting your reader know about your character. Read over your draft and search for places where you give the reader evidence. You may want to try some of the ideas from the chart we made in reading.

Writing Samples

Jackson taps in to his insights about character to develop a more robust sense of the character he is creating for his story (see Figure 12.2).

Lluvia has selected Ms. Penley as her character. She draws upon insights from our previous lessons and makes a sketch to help her visualize the character. Then she makes a list of the things she wants her readers to know about that character (see Figure 12.3).

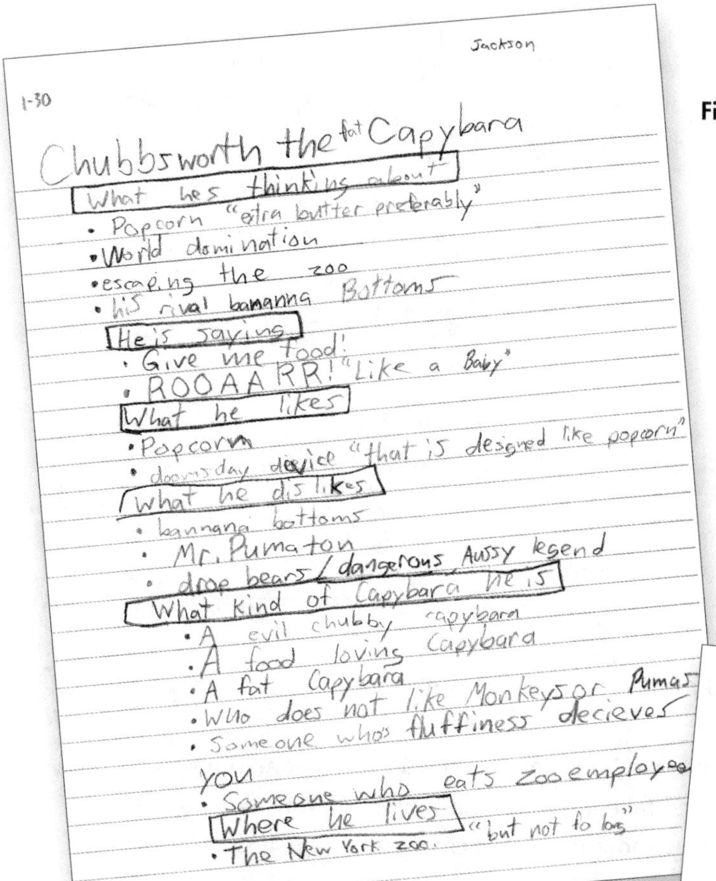

Jackson

1-30

Chubbsworth the fat Capybara

What he's thinking about
- Popcorn "extra butter preferably"
- World domination
- escaping the zoo
- his rival bananna Bottoms

He is saying
- Give me food!
- ROOAARR! "Like a Baby"

What he likes
- Popcorn
- doomsday device "that is designed like popcorn"

What he dislikes
- bannana bottoms
- Mr. Puma ton
- drop bears / dangerous Aussy legend

What kind of Capybara he is
- A evil chubby capybara
- A food loving Capybara
- A fat Capybara
- Who does not like Monkeys or Pumas
- Some one whos fluffiness decieves you
- Some one who eats zoo employees

Where he lives
- The New York Zoo. "but not fo long"

Figure 12.2 Jackson, Fifth Grade

I Like mrs. Penley she Reads the best books in the hole Wald. she Reads about dragons. She Reads to us out of the tubs. There name are Research, Fall Autumn Hallowean Familiey Read Aloud. She Reads books from home. we Like them a lot We like evrthing she does for us.

Figure 12.3 Lluvia, Second Grade (ELL student)

Florence writes about the year her baby sister was born and reveals much about herself. The reader can easily come to the end of this text and finish the sentence: "Florence is the kind of girl who . . ." (see Figure 12.4).

Florence → 5th

Little Sisters...

It was that year when my baby sister katie Elizabeth was born. I remember that day perfectly like it was yesterday. The first day was OK but the second day uhhh all my parents had all there attention to katie Elizabeth not once it it was about me. all I know was that I would never steal someones spotlight ok ok one time. Later that day the whole family came over for dinner that night. Everyone crowded around the baby except for me I was to busy planning revenge to get that baby out of the ballpark. When it was time to go dinner we all sat down and once katie Elezibeth cough they all laughed and smile at her but when I coughed the said "cover your mouth". It got to the

Figure 12.4 Florence, Fifth Grade

point where I couldn't handle it anymore. So after dinner I went upstairs brush my teeth packed my bag and went to the dog house were little Sammy lives. After about 2 hours I got really bored and Sammy smelled had a stitch to him that wasn't all that pleasant. so I came in. Everyone was wondering were I was and that the were nervous about me. Grammy came in the room carrying katie Elizabeth in her arms. "Catherine do you want to hold your baby sister?" said Grammy. Everyone was looking at me like go hold your little sister so I said yes. Once I got to hold katie Elizabeth I was so excited to be a big sister. And thats story about my little sister.

Additional Texts: Character

An Angel for Solomon Singer by Cynthia Rylant: There are two strong characters closely aligned in this plot. Solomon, a farmer from Indiana, has moved to New York City and is very lonely. He misses everything about his home in Indiana. He meets a waiter named Angel who greets him with a smile every night as he enters the café. Solomon soon becomes familiar with his new surroundings, and while he still misses Indiana he begins to feels at home. That transformation began with the warmth of a smile from Angel.

Charlotte's Web by E. B. White: This story is an unmatched text for studying the development of characters. White reveals the drama Wilbur feels when Charlotte begins to fade from life after her babies are born. He uses rich language to reveal the legacy of Charlotte's generous nature. Even the members of the Arable family are developed with specific traits that help the reader see the role each of them plays as the plot unfolds.

The Great Gilly Hopkins by Katherine Paterson: Gilly, an eleven-year-old foster child, is out to offend each new host family before they can request she be moved from their house. Her defense mechanism leaves evidence of poor choices and unacceptable behavior in each chapter. Equally well developed is the character of Maime Trotter, Gilly's guardian in her current foster home. Overweight, insightful, and generous are just three of the traits that describe the nearly illiterate Maime Trotter. Then there is the seven-year-old William Ernest, afraid of the brilliant Gilly who picks on him constantly, causing one disaster after another. These characters will have readers cheering for Gilly as she foolishly causes havoc in an attempt to cover up her true feelings and cheering for Ms. Trotter as she plods along, reassuring Gilly that she does belong.

When Jessie Came Across the Sea by Amy Hest: Jessie is an unforgettable character who lives with her grandmother and learns to sew fine laces by hand. When the opportunity arises for someone to travel to America, the rabbi selects the orphan, Jessie. Leaving her beloved grandmother breaks Jessie's heart, but once aboard the ship she dries her tears and begins to help others with her sewing skills. When she arrives in New York City, her skills become well known, and after several years of sewing and saving her coins she earns enough to purchase a ticket for her grandmother to join her in America.

With Books and Bricks: How Booker T. Washington Built a School by Suzanne Slade: This story tells of a young slave boy who wants to learn to read. From sunrise to sunset he worked, regardless of the task given him. When Booker was nine years old, the Civil War ended, freeing the slaves. As he grew older Booker took job after job, moving him closer and closer to his dream of an education. In Virginia, he attended college and graduated in only three years. He was invited to travel and teach in Tuskegee, Alabama, but once he reached the town he found no school. He found only children wanting an education. Rather than giving up, he set his sight on building a school brick by brick.

13

SETTING

Life doesn't happen in a vacuum. It happens in the grocery store and in the closet, storing away clothes from last season. Life happens in shadows and bright light and in the twinkle-glow of candles. It happens in a blizzard and while eating a Blizzard. It happens with salt spray and sand and the smell of sunscreen accompanied by the rhythmic drone of waves finding the shoreline. Life happens with the drip of an IV bag, the smell of coffee, the cries of a baby in another room. Life happens in a moment, across moments, every moment in places with light and sound, tastes and aromas and atmosphere. Life happens in settings. Things happen at the beach that don't happen in the office. The weather affects our choice of clothing. The formality of the event sets a tone for the interaction of the guests. Shouting is appropriate in a football stadium. Soft voices are expected in the ICU at the hospital. Setting influences everything, and story, like life, happens in a setting.

◄ LESSON FOCUS Exploring Setting as Readers

Readers, we've been exploring how the elements of story help us make sense of what we read and inform our writing. Today we are going to explore the important role of setting and how writers help us know where the story is taking place. Setting is more than the location; it's also about the time, and the weather, and what the character smells and hears and tastes and feels.

Today we are going to revisit one of our best friend books, *Apt. 3*, written and illustrated by Ezra Jack Keats.

[Present the front cover.]

We know that Sam and his little brother Ben hear harmonica music in their building, and they set out to find where it is coming from. We know what they discover as they make their way through the apartment building. We know they meet the blind man who lives in apartment 3 and become friends with him. So today as I read, I want you to focus on the setting. Move along with Sam and Ben, and notice what is around them, notice what they see and hear and smell and feel. Think about how the surroundings make you feel. Think about what Ezra does with his words to help us know what it is like to be there.

Because we have read this story before, we know everything is happening in an apartment building in the city, so focus your attention on the feel of the place. Think about how it sounds and smells. Think about whether it is bright or dark and whether it is happy or sad or creepy. I would say it like this: "Sam and Ben are in the kind of place where . . ."

I'll read the first few pages and show you what I mean.

[Read the first three spreads.]

Sam and Ben are in the kind of place where

- there are tall buildings in the city.

- there are several apartments in their building.

- you can see and hear the rain.

- you can hear music in the building.

- you can hear rain and city sounds outside the building.

- the weather and sounds make them have a sad and lonely feeling.

- they can hear sounds from inside apartments as they pass by each door.

I know these things because Ezra Jack Keats

- describes the weather ("the rain fell steadily").

- explains the sound of the rain ("it beat against the windows, softening the sounds of the city.").

- uses sound words to let us hear inside an apartment ("Crunch, crackle, crunch!").

I'll read a few more pages, then pause and ask you to talk with your partner about the setting and how Ezra helps us to know what it is like.

[Read the next four spreads, and stop when Sam and Ben reach the ground floor.]

Readers, sit with these pages for a moment. What are you noticing about the setting? How does Ezra take us into the place with Ben and Sam?

[Pause briefly.]

Share your thoughts and your evidence with your partner.

[Pause briefly.]

Let's hear from a few of you.

Sam and Ben are in the kind of place where

- ⬍ they live on the fourth floor in the building.
- ⬍ there are three apartments on each floor.
- ⬍ some things need repair.
- ⬍ people put their old stuff in the hall.
- ⬍ you can have a dog in your apartment.
- ⬍ you can smell cooking and cigarettes from other apartments.
- ⬍ where people smoke cigarettes in their apartments.
- ⬍ you can hear other people talk and sing and shout when you're in the hall.
- ⬍ there is a super who is supposed to fix things but he doesn't.

We know this because

- ⬍ the narrator tells us what they smell as they pass each door.
- ⬍ the narrator tells us what they hear from the hallway.
- ⬍ the narrator tells us how many times they went down the steps to the next floor.
- ⬍ the narrator tell us the apartment numbers on each floor.
- ⬍ Ben and Sam talk about what they hear and smell.

[Continue to the end of the book repeating the process above.]

Now let's think about how it feels for Ben and Sam. Think about what it looks like. Does the place help them or get in their way? Talk with your partner about that.

[Pause briefly.]

Let's hear your thinking.

- ◆ It's kind of creepy because it's dark on one floor and they are sneaking around.
- ◆ The rain and the music and the dark hallway and the smells and sounds make it feel a little scary or creepy.
- ◆ It feels like a mystery, like they might get caught doing something sneaky.

We are noticing several details in the writing that help us know what the place feels like and what Sam and Ben may be feeling as they search for the music they hear. This lets us know that setting is often much more than just "the place where the story happens." In this story, the setting helps create the feeling we get as we read.

So readers, let's summarize what we have discovered today about how we come to know about the setting. [Make note of their thinking and create a chart after the lesson.]

We learn about the setting when

- ◆ the narrator describes the location or environment (five senses).
- ◆ the narrator allows us to sense what the character senses (five senses).
- ◆ the character reacts to a sensory detail (smiles, winces, holds his nose, covers his ears).
- ◆ the narrator describes the weather (rain, cold, wind, sunny, hot, snow).
- ◆ the narrator describes the environment (apartment house, city, village, mountains, marsh, beach, desert).
- ◆ the character reacts to the weather or environment (shivers, sweats, puts on a coat, gets an umbrella, builds a fire, opens the windows, packs a compass and extra supplies).
- ◆ the character's actions are influenced by the weather or environment (seeks shelter, stays indoors, finds a shady spot in the park).

Today as you move out to your reading spot, I'd like you to pause a moment before you begin. Hold the book you are reading and think about the setting. Try to finish this sentence, "So this is happening in the kind of place where . . ." Then as you read, notice how the setting helps make the story.

Flip It from Reading to Writing

As readers we get drawn into the story; we move in alongside the character as he navigates his landscape. It is possible that we aren't even conscious of how that happens, but it is triggered by what the writer sets up. As writers we have to know the landscape our character will navigate. We have to know whether he will take the stairs or the elevator. We have to know if there is a big dog on the block that frightens him and how the rain makes him feel. We have to know if a blizzard is in the forecast or if he's living through a five-year drought. We have to know if he takes the bus to school or rides a bike or goes in a carpool. Setting is more than where the story happens. Setting is the place (mountains, Greece, Iowa, Beaufort, Biltmore Avenue, home, school playground, dentist's office), the time (winter, morning, 4:37 p.m., long ago when there were dragons), and the environment (foggy, thunderstorm, drought, 107 degrees, dark and dank, creepy, the aroma of fresh bread, suspenseful, the incessant squeak of old machinery, a creaking stair tread). Setting is the character's world, and it influences his thinking, his obstacles, his options, his actions, and his reactions. Setting is an essential element for writers to develop, yet it is often overlooked or perhaps just assumed in the drafts of many young writers.

⊟ LESSON FOCUS Exploring Setting as Writers

Writers, we've been exploring how the different elements of a story work together to help us as readers. Recently we explored how the setting can influence what the characters do and how they make decisions. We examined how writers use details about the setting to help us understand how it feels to be where the character is.

Today we are going to explore how we can flip those understandings over and bring them into our writing. First we have to think about our character and what we know about him. Part of what we know is where he is and how that place or situation makes a difference.

Let me show you what I mean. A few days ago we were working to develop our characters and help the reader get to know them. One day I showed you a page from my notebook where I was brainstorming ideas about a pig named William that I want to write about. Now I'm thinking about him and the story I want to write, and I need to think about the setting for that story. I went back to my notes about William last night, and I added ideas about the setting. [See Figure 13.1.]

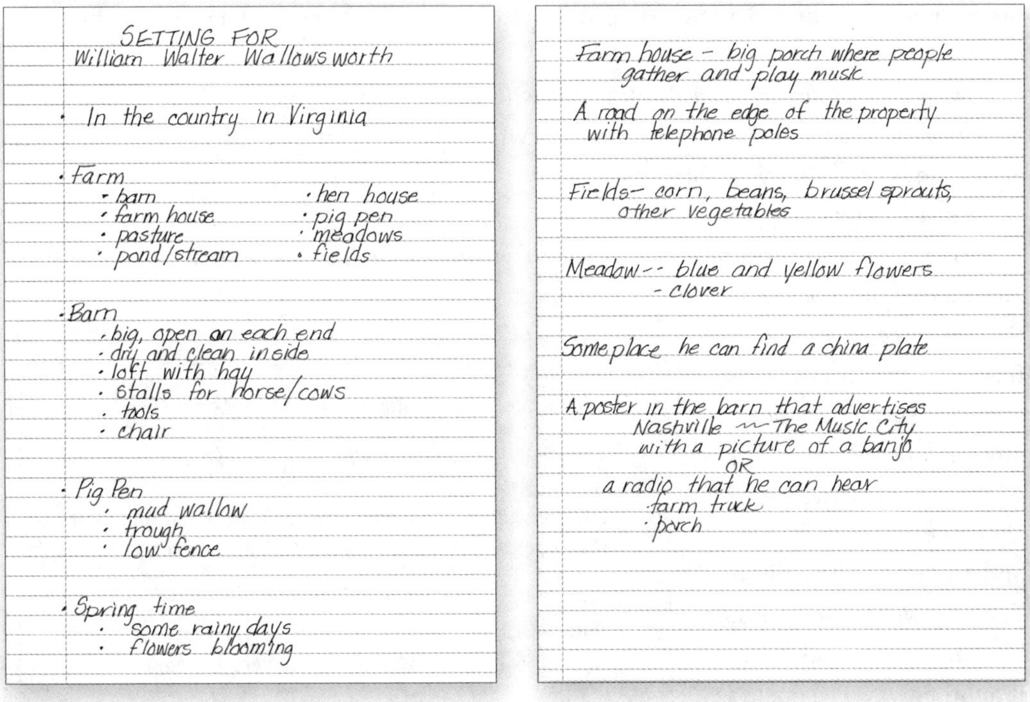

Figure 13.1 Setting for William Walter Wallowsworth

When I reviewed my notes on William I noticed some things right away. This story will happen on a farm in Virginia, so I wrote that in my notebook. Then I thought about what William would see on the farm, and I made a list.

Next I thought about the places he would spend most of his time. His world would be the barn and the pigpen and maybe the meadow, so I added some details to each of those. Since William doesn't like to get dirty, the barn can be a dry and clean place for him to go. Since the other pigs tease him, they need a muddy pigpen to wallow in. And it needs to be spring so William can see the clover and flowers in the meadow. I added a big porch on the farmhouse so there is a place where people can make music and he can see and hear them. Each detail I'm adding to my notes for the setting is connected to what I know about William.

These details may change as I begin to draft the story, but for now this helps me get focused.

Writers, let's try this out. Think about the story you are working on now and the notes you made about your main character. Review those notes and search for any connection to his setting. Then turn to a new page, and write the word *Setting* at the top. Put that character's name there also.

Now pause a moment and think about where this character will be. Think about what he will see and do and the time of year and what he hears. Jot down a couple of thoughts about the setting that you notice right away.

[Pause briefly.]

Writers, today as you move out to your writing spot, I'd like you to try something. Sit with your notebook open to this page, and take a few more minutes to think about the setting. Jot down any other details you think of about the setting. Think about the place and the time and the feel of the place. You may write it in lists as I did in my notebook or try it another way. I've made a chart to remind us what we learned about setting. This chart may help you get focused.

After that I'd like you to return to your draft and look for places where you are letting the reader know what it feels like to be where your character is. You may want to try some of the ideas from the chart we made in reading.

We help our readers understand the setting when we

- describe the location or environment (five senses)

- let the reader know what character senses and noting which sense is a logical focus in this context (five senses)

- show how the character reacts to a sensory detail (smiles, winces, holds his nose, covers his ears)

- describe the weather (rain, cold, wind, sunny, hot, snow)

- describe the environment (apartment house, city, village, mountains, marsh, beach, desert)

- show how character reacts to the weather or environment (shivers, sweats, puts on a coat, gets an umbrella, builds a fire, opens the windows, packs a compass and extra supplies)

- show how the character's actions are influenced by the weather or environment (seeks shelter, stays indoors, finds a shady spot in the park)

Writing Samples

Jazlyn gets her thoughts together for a "Where I'm From" poem by making a list of what is most important about her hometown (see Figure 13.2).

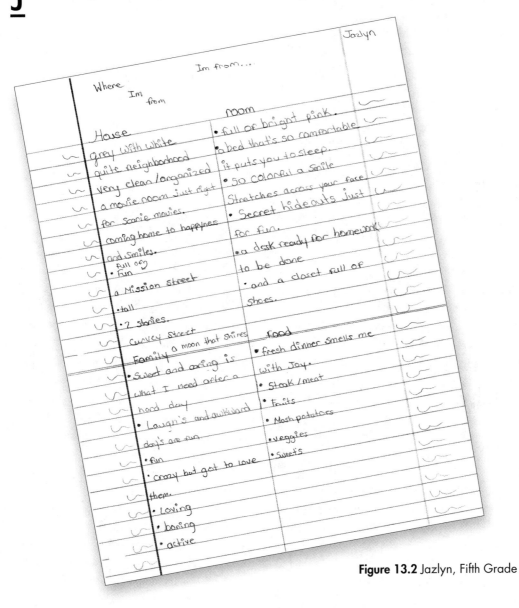

Figure 13.2 Jazlyn, Fifth Grade

Chase uses specific details and dialog to bring his readers into the setting (see Figure 13.3).

Chase B

My happiest time

"AHH HH" I said as I sat on the edge of my bed I'm so lucky I said to myself as I bounced on the bed I "own" in Florida (It's my grandmothers, guest bedroom bed).The sun was already shining at 8:00 am. in Sarasota, Florida.

"Morning everyone. After breakfast may I take a swim?"

"Sure, as long as you put your sunscreen on."

After an expertly cooked breakfast (cooked by Master chef Meme) I put on my sunscreen and jumped in the pool.My dad walked out and asked."Think you can catch a tennis ball while jumping into a pool?"

"Easily" I replied.

So I ran and leaped high as I could, and SPLASH! Although I couldn't see I didn't feel a ball in

my hand. I exploded through the surface looking to see where the tennis ball landed. I didn't see it anywhere?

"Looking for this?" my dad asked holding a bright neon yellow ball. I climbed my way out of the pool, grabbed a noodle and shouted "After you arm yourself, meet me in the shallow end for a noodle fight!"

Figure 13.3 Chase, Fifth Grade

Additional Texts: Setting

All the Places to Love by Patricia MacLachlan: When Eli was born his grandmother held him in the open window so he could hear the wind and see all the places to love. Each person in his life had one favorite place on the farm. As he grew he was introduced to each one and came to understand that no matter where he went in life, all the places to love would always be here on the farm. The text reads beautifully as MacLachlan describes each of the places. The tradition continues as Eli and his family welcome a baby sister.

BigMama's by Donald Crews: This memoir recounts Crews' visits to his grandmother's home each summer. The text begins with the family traveling to reach the house where BigMama is waiting for them with big hugs and kisses. Every detail of the book works to develop the setting with descriptions of things found only at BigMama's (i.e., a sewing machine you had to pedal, a wind-up record player, a well where you got your water and drank out of a dipper, the Sears and Roebuck catalogue, and an outhouse). Crews weaves in rich descriptions of the setting as the children run around the yard to rediscover all their favorite things from last summer's visit.

Roller Coaster by Marla Frazee: The author brings the reader along on a first roller coaster ride. Readers are taken from standing in line, to buckling in, to slowly ascending the steep hill and all that follows, to walking off the ride and wanting to ride again. While the setting could be any amusement park, the emotions and tension are specific to riding a roller coaster.

Sequoia by Tony Johnston: This book uses personification to tell readers the life of the evergreen sequoia tree. In lyrical language Johnston describes the life for the largest tree on Earth, which is found on the California and Nevada border in a distinct area along the western side of the Sierra Nevada range.

14

PLOT

L ife unfolds like a story. Everything moves along and seems to be unfolding like a plan
when an unexpected twist presents us with drama, a dilemma, or a challenge and
pushes us to make decisions that impact our actions. There is change as you work to
solve the problems.

Life is story, and story must have a plot.

Plot in many ways is the plan (the road map) the story will follow from beginning
through the middle to a logical conclusion at the end. The typical plot structure includes
exposition, rising action, falling action, and denouement. The exposition opens the story
with description and explanation, giving the reader a sense of the people and place. In
short, the exposition sets the stage. The rising action sets the story in motion with a series
of events where the main character's conflict or obstacle becomes clear and something
must be done to resolve it. The falling action brings us down from the drama of meeting
the conflict and working toward some closure. The denouement, the bow on a package,
wraps things up nicely, bringing a sense of resolution or closure.

Coming to understand how story is put together helps us as readers to recognize how
characters and settings and plot interact. When those concepts become part of our background knowledge and schema, we open a story with a sense of the familiar, a sense of
expectation that makes for more efficient and engaged reading.

Readers, we have been exploring how the elements of story help us to make sense as we read. Today we are going to focus on plot. A plot is what happens in a story. Plot is the main events without all the little details, almost like an outline or a map.

Let's think of a birthday party. Most of us know what to expect when we go to a birthday party. There will be decorations and a birthday cake with candles and presents for the birthday person.

Many things can happen, but the plot for most birthday parties goes something like this: In the beginning people bring presents and sing happy birthday. Then in the middle the birthday person blows out candles and makes a wish. Everyone eats cake and ice cream. And at the end the birthday person is excited and is eager to open the presents and find out what is inside each one. The birthday person opens presents. Everyone plays games and goes home.

The plot is like a map that shows the main parts—the beginning and the middle and the end. So today I'm going to revisit a book we know very well, *Peter's Chair* by Ezra Jack Keats. I'll read it all the way through without stopping. As I'm reading I'd like you to focus your attention on the plot of this story. When we reach the end I'll ask you to talk with your partner and identify the parts of the plot.

[Remember to hold the book so children are able to see the illustrations as you read the story at a normal pace.]

Readers, pause a moment. Sit with the story and think about the plot: the beginning, and then the middle, and finally the end.

[Pause briefly.]

Turn and share your thoughts with your partner.

[Pause briefly.]

Readers, I've been listening and it seems most of you are saying the plot for this story is

> **Beginning**—Peter's mother warns him to play quietly because there is a new baby in the house.
>
> **Middle**—Peter notices all his old baby things are being painted pink for his new sister. He gets jealous and takes a chair they haven't painted yet and he runs away.
>
> **End**—Peter realizes he has grown and no longer needs those baby things and returns home to help his dad paint the chair.

In the next few days we will revisit other books and think about the plot in each story. Today as you move out to read, think about the plot for the story you are reading.

Readers, yesterday we revisited *Peter's Chair* with our focus on finding the plot and seeing the plan for the story. We identified the beginning, middle, and end. Today we are going to think a bit more about the plot for *Peter's Chair*. The plot of a story has a spot in the middle where the main character has to solve a problem or resolve a conflict. Then the rest of the story is about finding a way to work it out.

I'm going to read the story again. As I read you think about the conflict or problem Peter is facing. And notice how he works it out.

[Read the story without stopping.]

I know we are all very familiar with the story, but I'd like you to sit with your thoughts a moment. Give your brain time to focus on exactly what you will say. Think about the conflict Peter was facing and how he worked it out.

[Pause briefly.]

Readers, share your thoughts with your partner.

[Pause briefly.]

So it seems there is agreement that the conflict Peter has to resolve is that he is jealous because his baby sister is getting all his old things and his father is painting them pink.

He worked that out by taking the chair and running away, only to realize he was too big for those things now. So he took the chair to his dad and helped him paint it pink.

Readers, today as you go out to read, think about the conflict your main character is facing and think about how the writer lets you know.

⟳ **Flip It from Reading to Writing**

As writers, the plot is our road map and our headlights as we navigate through the story. The seed idea for a story may begin with an event or a character, but the writer will have to devise a plot to move the story along without meandering aimlessly and placing our readers in a state of utter confusion. Plans for the plot may evolve and change over time as the writer generates a draft and rewrites and revises.

⊟ LESSON FOCUS Exploring Plot as Writers

Writers, in our reading work we have been exploring how plot helps us make sense. We determined that plot is like a map of the story showing what happens in the main parts from the beginning to the end. We see the plot unfold as we read. The plot helps us create a concise summary of the story. But when we write, we have to devise the plot ourselves. As writers we plan the big chunks of the story to keep us focused and on topic.

Today we are going to begin exploring plot as writers. If the plot is like a map for the big events in the story, we could flip that idea and use it as a plan for our writing.

You've been helping me think about the story I want to write about a pig that doesn't like mud. I showed you my notes for the character, William Walter Wallowsworth. And I showed you the notes I made when thinking about the farm where he lives. Before I begin to draft the story, I have to think about the plot.

Last night I made a few notes in my notebook. Let's take a look, and I'll tell you what I was thinking. [See Figure 14.1.]

I looked back at my notebook and reviewed what I wrote about William and the setting. Since he likes the meadow and blue and yellow flowers I decided to begin with his happy place. And I know he prefers dinner on a china plate and he likes banjo music. So I decided to have him dreaming about those things.

So the beginning gives you an idea of what William is like.

In our reading work we discovered that the middle is usually where the character has some kind of problem or obstacle to work out. We know that William does not like mud or getting dirty, so in the middle I'm going to have a big thunderstorm come and turn the barnyard into a muddy mess. That gives him a problem for getting back inside. Then the other pigs tease him about that and make it worse.

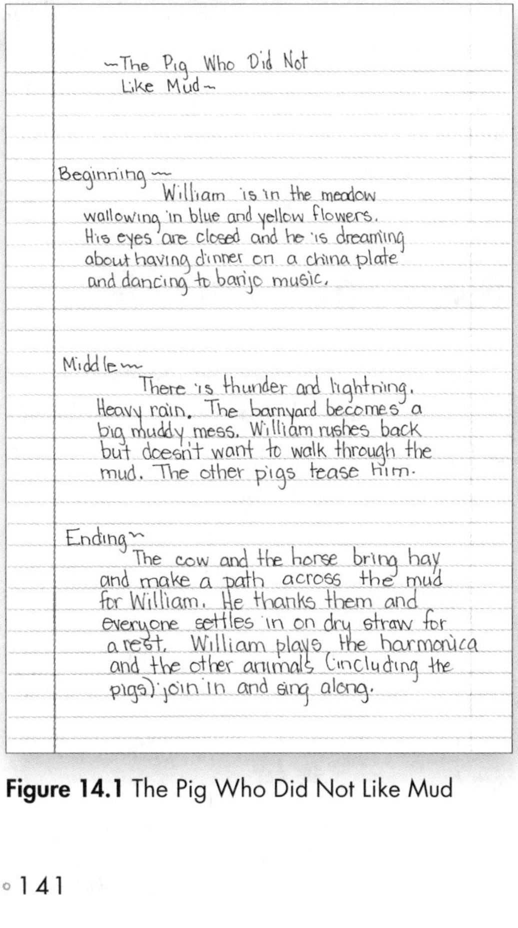

~The Pig Who Did Not Like Mud~

Beginning ~
    William is in the meadow wallowing in blue and yellow flowers. His eyes are closed and he is dreaming about having dinner on a china plate and dancing to banjo music.

Middle ~
    There is thunder and lightning. Heavy rain. The barnyard becomes a big muddy mess. William rushes back but doesn't want to walk through the mud. The other pigs tease him.

Ending ~
    The cow and the horse bring hay and make a path across the mud for William. He thanks them and everyone settles in on dry straw for a rest. William plays the harmonica and the other animals (including the pigs) join in and sing along.

Figure 14.1 The Pig Who Did Not Like Mud

We know that the ending has to give us some kind of a solution or resolution that wraps up the story so I'm going to have the cow and the horse make a path of hay for William to get back safely inside.

So, writers, see how the notes about my character and the setting helped me think about the plot? Of course, that can change as I begin to draft the story, but it gives me a good focus to begin writing.

Take a moment and open your notebook to the pages where you've been planning your next story. Look over your notes about your character and the setting. Think about the plot. What will need to happen in the beginning to get the story going? What will be the conflict or problem your character has to resolve? What will happen to resolve the problem and bring the story to a close?

[Pause briefly as students review their notes.]

Now, turn to your partner and share a few of your thoughts.

[Allow time for each partner to share briefly.]

Writers, as you go out to write I'd like you to continue thinking about the ideas you've shared with your partners. Remember to look back at your notes about your character and the setting. Then use information from those notes to begin making notes about the plot. For the plot you'll want to think about a beginning, middle, and end to your story and make a decision about when a conflict or tension arises and gets resolved. Let's go write!

Writing Sample

Lucas brings his reader–knowledge about character and setting and plot together in this piece as he builds tension and brings the reader along to his exciting closure (see Figure 14.2).

PROLOGUE

I tapped my pencil to my chin. "Hmmmm..." I thought. "What should it be about? I asked.

"What about why did the whale cross the ocean?..." my mom said.

"No, it has to be original". And then it hit me, the perfect joke.

* * * * *

"MOOOOOMMM!" I yelled. "I'm going out to check the mail again."

"OK! But be careful!" She said.

"I will!" As I ran down the gravel driveway to the mail box, I thought about that cold day in January when I found the perfect joke. I had sent it to boys life magazine headquarters in Austin, Texas. I opened the mailbox hesitantly. There were many letters inside, but none addressed to me. I frowned. This was my last chance.

Then, all of sudden, a blue envelope that I hadn't seen before fell out.

Figure 14.2 Lucas, Fifth Grade

I picked it up, but when I saw what was on it I almost fainted. It was addressed to Lucas C. of Bethel. And on it was Pedro the whaky Mailburro. My jaw dropped at that. I gawked at that letter like my lip was weighted.

I opened it right away. Enclosed was a ten dollars and a note. The note said,

"Dear Lucas,

We are thankful that you sent your joke to us. It was wonderful! It will be in the March 2014 issue. (Pleas use the ten dollars enclosed to buy we an alfalfa milkshake :))

Yours,

UUPEDRO

the wacky mail burro"

I sprinted up to the house, waving the envelope high above my head. My sisters were laying on the ground, and I hurtled over them.

"Hey! watch it!" Ella yelled.

"I DID IT MOMMA! I DID IT!

I'M FAMOUS!" I screamed.

"Whoa! Slow down. What did you do?" She said calmly.

I shoved the blue note into her hands. Her lips moved as she read it. Her eyes widened. She handed it back to me and ran over to the phone. She pressed in a number.

"Tell him!" she said.

I told my dad the news.

"Woohoo!" He yelled.

"You know what this means?" He said after we calmed down.

"What?"

"You have a future in writing."

"Then thats what I'll do!"

I smiled, and I could tell that he did too.

Additional Texts: Plot

Enemy Pie by Derek Munson: Our narrator was set up for the perfect summer because his dad had built a tree house, he was on the best baseball team, and his sister was away for summer camp. The tension rises when Jeremy Ross moves into the neighborhood, and the perfect summer evaporates. The plot thickens when our narrator declares his first official enemy. Dad comes up with the perfect solution: Feed him a slice of enemy pie. The plot moves toward a peaceful resolution when Dad announces that our narrator must spend one day playing with his enemy (Jeremy) to make the pie effective. After spending one day playing and even allowing Jeremy into his beloved tree house, our narrator had changed (just as Dad had predicted).

Erika's Story by Ruth Vander Zee: This story offers readers a small window into the horrors of the Holocaust. Erika was only an infant in 1944 when her mother and father were packed into a railroad car to move them from a ghetto in the city to the Dachau concentration camp for certain death. While packed into the railroad car with standing room only, the parents made the heart-breaking decision to wrap their tiny baby in jackets from passengers and toss her into the grass at a crossing in hopes that a woman would not let a baby suffer. Erika was discovered by a German woman who risked her own safety to save the baby. She gave the tiny baby girl a name (Erika) and a birth date. Woven throughout Erika's story are facts about the Holocaust and how at least six million people were killed. As a grown woman, Erika told this story to the author.

Feathers and Fools by Mem Fox: This picture book features a complex plot showing how distrust often stems from deeper evil thoughts. If not addressed, those thoughts may manifest as hostile behavior. The plot begins with swans and peacocks living peacefully around a lake until one day the peacocks began noticing the difference between them and the swans. Soon the swans were doing the same. Eventually doubt and anxious mutterings result in a master plan for each flock to rid the lake of the other. The distrust escalates until all that remains is one egg from each flock. When the eggs hatched and tiny birds emerged, they focused on their similarities rather than their differences, and a new friendship was begun.

Grandfather's Journey by Allen Say: The author recounts the story of his grandfather leaving Japan as a young man to come to America. He tells us of his grandfather's deep abiding love for both countries and their customs. When he was in either country he longed for the beauty of the other. In short lines, Allen provides a comprehensive look through his grandfather's eyes at the expanse and features of America. Eventually the grandfather returns to Japan to raise his daughter who became the mother to Allen. His grandfather's stories about America planted seeds in the young boy's mind, leading him to make his own journey many years later.

15

PERSPECTIVE AND
POINT OF VIEW

Throughout our lives we face challenges and hardships, struggles, triumphs and successes. We win. We lose. We love, and we hurt. We gather, collect, sort, and purge. We buy. We sell. We toss out. Each event in life is deemed either good or bad or neutral. Decisions are deemed right or wrong. Material possessions, places, relationships, and experiences are valued as positive or negative. The events of our lives are experienced and valued from a perspective. We perceive life through a lens created by our knowledge and understandings, our culture, religion and politics, our beliefs and values.

To gain a bit of perspective on perspective, think about an old chair found in a thrift shop. For one person that chair is the best find of the year, and to another it is just an old chair no one wants. Perspective.

Two people approach a parking space from different directions. One speeds up and zips in the spot thinking himself bold and aggressive. The other one moves cautiously down the row of spaces thinking what a jerk that other driver was. Perspective.

An old house in much need of repair comes on the market for sale. One person sees an opportunity to purchase the house at a good price, update it, and flip it. Another person sees a total disaster and can't imagine why anyone would want such a mess. Perspective.

Our notions of good and bad, value and worth, truth and justice, equity and fairness come down to perspective. The ability to see or feel or think of an event from a different perspective allows us to broaden our understanding. As readers we seek to recognize the perspective through which the story is being told. A critical reader will question that perspective and consider how the perspective slants the story, perhaps even wondering how the story would be different from a different perspective.

Story is told through a perspective and through a point of view. Consider an eightieth birthday celebration for a great-grandfather. In attendance are friends and neighbors, siblings and children, grandchildren and great-grandchildren. In the weeks that follow, the party is recounted again and again by various guests. It isn't difficult to imagine the difference in the story told by the great-grandfather and one told by a great-grandchild. And both those versions would differ from that of a neighbor. Each of these individuals will speak to similar events, but the details will be filtered through his particular perspective.

Point of view, though often used as a synonym for perspective, is something different. Point of view is the stance taken by the narrator, whether the narrator is speaking as the character in first person, placing you (the reader) in the story in second person, or stepping back and speaking in third person, able to see everything going on and giving the reader that same view.

Perspective and point of view are necessarily connected. The story is told through a perspective (e.g., the great-grandfather's view) and from a point of view (first-, second-, or third-person). For example, if the birthday story mentioned above were told from the great-grandfather's perspective using a first-person point of view, we hear him tell what happened, what he noticed, and how he felt about it. If the story were told from the great-grandfather's perspective using a second-person point of view, we would hear the narrator telling us (the reader) how to have a wonderful eightieth birthday party. And if the story were told from the great-grandfather's perspective using a third-person (limited) point of view, the narrator would tell us everything that happened. We may see things the great-grandfather doesn't see, but we would be allowed to know only his thoughts and feelings. A third-person (omniscient) point of view would enable the narrator to provide the reader access to the thoughts and feelings of others as well.

✏ LESSON FOCUS Introduce the Concept of Perspective and Point of View

Let's imagine there was a big parade and lots of people were there. After the parade was over the lady on the news came by with her microphone and talked with three people. One person was a three-year-old boy who had to stand behind a group of grownups wearing big coats. The second person was a grandfather who watched the parade with his granddaughter from the window of his apartment. And the third person was a teenager who played a trumpet in one of the bands that marched in the parade.

All three people were at the same parade, but each one would have something different to tell because each one had a different perspective, and each has had different experiences with parades. So each person has a different perspective. For example, the grandfather watching through the window in his apartment has probably watched several parades. He knows what to look for. From his window he can see a whole block at one time. But the three-year-old has never been to a parade, and he doesn't know what it is. He can't see much. He sees coats and shoes and legs. He hears music and drums and people. And the teenager plays a trumpet in the band. He has marched in many parades, but this is a really big parade, and he sees all the people on the street. He watches the director to know when to march and what to play. Each person would have a story to tell about the parade, but now we know that each perspective will make the story very different.

Stories also have a point of view.

- ◆ First person: If the grandfather tells a story about the parade and tells what he saw and what he was thinking and what he felt, that would be first person. He is telling it himself, and he would say something like, "Yesterday when I was watching the parade I saw the biggest balloon ever. My granddaughter loved watching with me."

- ◆ Second person: But if a teenager was telling his cousin how to plan for a parade, he might say, "When you make plans to attend a parade there are several important things to consider. First you should arrive early and pick a spot. And, of course, you will want to make sure small children will be able to see everything so pick a spot up front." When the storyteller has you as part of the story, the point of view is called second person.

- ◆ Third person: There is one more point of view, called third person. That's when the storyteller (narrator) can see everything. The news reporter saw the whole parade and moved around talking with people, so when she does a story on the news that night she will be telling about the parade. She may decide to focus on the three-year-old boy and tell us all about what happened in the parade and what everyone saw, but she decides to take her camera and sit down next to the boy so we hear all the music and drums and the noise of the crowd, but we see coats and legs and only a few things passing by between the people standing in front of us. Her story lets us see the parade the way a small boy would see it.

In the next few days we will revisit some books we've read and explore how perspective helps us make sense of what we read.

◄ LESSON FOCUS Exploring Perspective as Readers

Readers, we've been exploring perspective and point of view and how that can help us make meaning. Today we are going to revisit a best friend book, *Trouper*, written by Meg Kearney and illustrated by E. B. Lewis. We know the story very well, so today we are going to think about two things. As I read I'd like you to think about whose perspective we are seeing the story from and which point of view it is told through.

When I reach the end of the story I'll ask you to think with your partner about the perspective and the point of view of the story.

[Read the story start to finish without stopping.]

Readers, think for a moment about this story and talk about which perspective we are given.

[Pause.]

It seems everyone is in agreement that we are seeing this story through the eyes of the dog, Trouper. Now I'd like you to pause a moment and think about when we are able to confirm that.

Let's move slowly through the pages and think about this.

[Hold the book so the art is visible and turn the pages slowly. Linger a few seconds with each page.]

Readers, from the very first page it is clear that a dog is telling the story, but we aren't certain which dog. There are several spreads where we can infer from the art that we are seeing this story from Trouper's perspective, but it isn't until this spread [Stop on the ninth spread where the boy is face to face with Trouper at the pound.] that we can prove it.

Let's think about what Meg Kearney did on this page that lets us be certain. I'll read these two pages again.

[Read this spread aloud.]

Talk with your partner.

[Pause briefly.]

On this page Meg Kearney has Trouper speaking directly to the boy. And in the art E. B. Lewis shows the boy and Trouper looking right at each other.

So the story is told from Trouper's perspective. Now take a moment and think with your partner about which point of view is used and how you know.

[Pause.]

I'm hearing agreement that the story is told from a first-person point of view. And we can prove that on the very first page.

[Return to the first page of the story and read it aloud.]

The narrator is speaking in an "I" voice, telling his own version of the story.

Readers, hearing this story from Trouper's perspective makes it different from most stories about adopting a dog. Think about how the story would have been different if the boy who adopted Trouper had told it. Or how it would have changed if told by the dog-catcher driving the truck. Perspective makes a big difference in how a story is told and how we make sense of it.

As you move out to read today, notice whose perspective you are seeing the story from and which point of view is being used. Think about how that perspective and point of view influence the meaning you make from the story.

Flip It from Reading to Writing

As readers, knowing about perspective helps us realize that the story has limitations. We will see what happens through a particular lens. Knowing that enables us to question what was not revealed. It also helps us to consider other characters and to recognize that each of them may have different views on the same events.

As writers we have to decide whose perspective will be the lens for our readers. We have to be conscious of how taking that perspective would influence what the reader is able to view, understand, believe, value, and share. As we tell the story, we have to be true to that lens. Then, as writers, we have to select the point of view that best enables us to reveal the story we want to share with our readers.

⊣ LESSON FOCUS Exploring Perspective as Writers

Writers, we have been thinking about how our reading insights can inform our writing work. Lately we've explored perspective and point of view in reading. Today we are going to begin thinking about how we can use those insights in our writing to help our readers make meaning.

Let's explore how a writer has to consider perspective and point of view. Think about the story you have been helping me get organized. We know the main character is William Walter Wallowsworth, and we know the setting is a farm in Virginia. We decided what would happen in the beginning and the middle and the end when we explored how writers think about plot. Now I have to decide whose perspective this story should be told through. We know William will be a character, and there will be other pigs, a horse, and a cow or two. There may be other farm animals and some people on the farm.

I could tell the story from the perspective of any of these characters. Take a moment and think about the decisions we made about character, setting, and plot. Use that knowledge and talk with your partner about which perspective makes the most sense for this story.

[Pause.]

Writers, thumbs up if you and your partner agree the story should be told through William's perspective. Well, that is almost everyone.

Now I have to decide which point of view to use. Should I write in first person, where William is telling you everything himself? Should I write in second person, where the narrator is including you in the story? Should I write in third person, where I can show you what everyone is doing and tell you what William is thinking and feeling? Sit with those options for a moment and think about yourself as a reader. Which one would help you make meaning and understand the story?

[Pause.]

Writers, share your thinking with your partner.

[Pause.]

It seems that most of you are suggesting I write in third person. I like that suggestion because writing this story in first person means that I could tell you only what William sees and thinks and feels. Writing in second person makes it more about you, the reader, and not as much about William and how he resolves the problem. I agree that writing in third person lets me show you more of what is happening all around the farm, even when William is away in the meadow. Then you'll understand what the cow and horse and other pigs are doing that help William or make a problem for him.

Writers, this has been very helpful today. Thank you for thinking about this with me.

Now, take a moment to think with your partner about the story you are planning. Which perspective and which point of view will work best for you?

[Pause briefly as they think and talk together.]

Writers, let's hear from a few of you.

[Allow a few students to share their thinking and offer a rationale for their decisions.]

Now as you move out to your writing today, I'd like you to return to your notes. Consider what you know about your character and the setting and the beginning, middle, and end in your plot. Today, jot a few notes about which perspective and what point of view will best match what you want to help your readers understand.

Writing Samples

Sherlyn, like many very young writers, writes from a personal perspective in a first-person point of view (see Figure 15.1). Early writing is often focused on sharing personal experiences and feelings.

Figure 15.1 Sherlyn, Kindergarten (ELL student)

Reagan writes from the perspective of her main character (Amelia) using a third-person point of view (see Figure 15.2).

Figure 15.2 Reagan, Fifth Grade

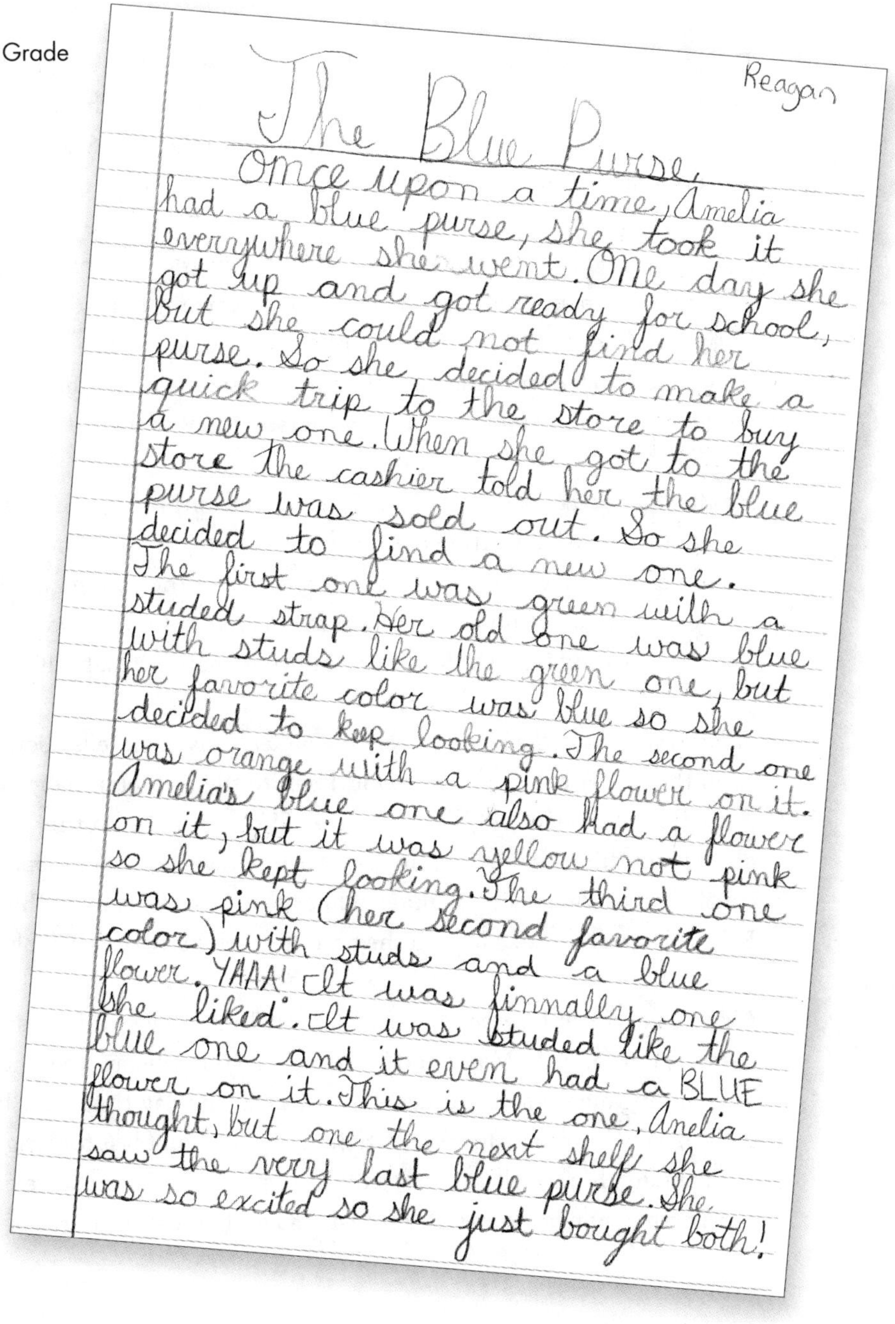

Reagan

The Blue Purse

Once upon a time, Amelia had a blue purse, she took it everywhere she went. One day she got up and got ready for school, but she could not find her purse. So she decided to make a quick trip to the store to buy a new one. When she got to the store the cashier told her the blue purse was sold out. So she decided to find a new one. The first one was green with a studed strap. Her old one was blue with studs like the green one, but her favorite color was blue so she decided to keep looking. The second one was orange with a pink flower on it. Amelia's blue one also had a flower on it, but it was yellow not pink so she kept looking. The third one was pink (her second favorite color) with studs and a blue flower. YAAA! It was finnally one she liked. It was studed like the blue one and it even had a BLUE flower on it. This is the one, Amelia thought, but one the next shelf she saw the very last blue purse. She was so excited so she just bought both!

Additional Texts: Perspective and Point of View

Do Not Open This Book! by Adam Lehrhaupt: This book is written from the second-person point of view, directing the reader to not open and read the book. Each page is filled with rollicking fun from the thrill of letting out monkeys and toucans and alligators. Young readers will hoot at each new adventure in this very short text.

Fifty Cents and a Dream: Young Booker T. Washington by Jabari Asim: This story is about a young boy born into slavery, whose dream of learning to read and write was against the law of the day. The story takes the reader through Booker's life as he moves from place to place in his quest to become an educated man who makes a difference for many young men and women. This story is told in the third-person point of view.

How to Babysit a Grandma by Jean Reagan: The author gives us the recipe for entertaining a grandma while babysitting her during an overnight visit. The story is told in the second-person point of view and from the perspective of the young granddaughter. Page by page the reader finds out how the girl entertains her grandma and how she can't wait for the next opportunity for a sleepover and another chance to babysit.

Julius: The Baby of the World by Kevin Henkes: This book tells about a young sister who has been the center of her parent's world before the arrival of baby Julius. Told in the third-person point of view, Lilly's perspective of her new baby brother is a negative one. She sees all the bad things happening in her world. However, that perspective changes when her cousin comes for a visit and finds Julius as disgusting as Lilly. The cousin's opinion causes Lilly's perspective to change as she becomes defensive of her baby brother.

Maple and Willow Together by Lori Nichols: This story of a friendship is told in the third-person point of view. Maple and Willow are sisters who are together all the time and really love playing all the same things, that is, until the day they can't bear to be together and are sent to their rooms for timeout. Being apart didn't last for long, and notes were passed back and forth until all anger was forgotten and the sisters were back together again. The perspective changes from sister to sister as each one is in charge of the activity for the day.

Secret Pizza Party by Adam Rubin: This story is told in the second-person point of view with lots of humor as a raccoon goes to great lengths to acquire slices of pizza. Equally devious are all the people who work through each scene to keep the raccoon away from the pizza. Readers will find themselves alternately cheering for the raccoon's success on one page and for the people on the next. Readers will delight in the adventures in this book.

A Sick Day for Amos McGee by Philip C. Stead: This tale told in the third-person point of view is about a zookeeper who loves his work and never misses a day. Amos treats every animal in his zoo as a friend and knows what each one needs. But one day Amos woke up with the sniffles and couldn't go see his friends at the zoo. By day's end the animals miss Amos so much they ride the bus to visit their friend. Amos's perspective from the beginning was shown through his knowledge of the needs of each of the animals under his care. When Amos gets sick the perspective changes and each of the animals reverses that knowledge to give to Amos the same things he had given to them.

A Sign by George Ella Lyon: This memoir picture book is told from the author's perspective in first person. As a young child in Kentucky, Lyon had many dreams for her future. Her first dreams were of making neon signs just like her neighbor. Then a trip to the circus led to dreams of becoming a tightrope walker. That passion faded when Alan Shepard went into outer space. These experiences led her to become the writer and poet we know today.

When Charley Met Grampa by Amy Hest: This story is written in the first-person point of view and tells the story of Henry, a young boy, and his dog, Charley. Henry's perspective in the story reveals his love for both Charley and his Grampa but also his concern since Grampa is not sure he likes dogs. Henry wants badly for the two loves of his life to like each other. On the trip home from meeting Grampa who came for his visit on the train, Grampa's cap blows off in the snow, and it is Charley to the rescue. From that moment on, Grampa and Charley become buddies.

WORKS CITED

Professional Literature

Fletcher, Ralph, and JoAnn Portalupi. 2007. *Craft Lessons: Teaching Writing K–8*. 2nd ed. Portland, ME: Stenhouse.

———. 2001. *Nonfiction Craft Lessons: Teaching Information Writing K–8*. Portland, ME: Stenhouse.

Keene, Ellin, and Susan Zimmermann. 2007. *Mosaic of Thought: The Power of Comprehension Strategy Instruction*. 2nd ed. Portsmouth, NH: Heinemann.

Laminack, Lester. 2007. *Cracking Open the Author's Craft: Teaching the Art of Writing*. New York: Scholastic.

———. 2009. *Unwrapping the Read Aloud: Making Every Read Aloud Intentional and Instructional*. New York: Scholastic.

Laminack, Lester, and Reba Wadsworth. 2006a. *Learning Under the Influence of Language and Literature: Making the Most of Read-Alouds Across the Day*. Portsmouth, NH: Heinemann.

———. 2006b. *Reading Aloud Across the Curriculum: How to Build Bridges in Language Arts, Math, Science, and Social Studies*. Portsmouth, NH: Heinemann.

———. 2013. *The Writing Teacher's Troubleshooting Guide*. Portsmouth, NH: Heinemann.

Ray, Katie Wood. 1999. *Wondrous Words: Writers and Writing in the Elementary School Classroom*. Urbana, IL: NCTE.

Children's Literature

Text Structure and Organization

DESCRIPTION

Brinckloe, Julie. 1986. *Fireflies!* New York: Simon and Schuster.

Fletcher, Ralph. 1997. *Twilight Comes Twice.* New York: Clarion.

MacLachlan, Patricia. 1994. *All the Places to Love.* New York: HarperCollins.

Rylant, Cynthia. 2008. *In November.* Boston: Harcourt.

Simon, Seymour. 2002. *Animals Nobody Loves.* San Francisco: Chronicle Books.

Yolen, Jane. 1987. *Owl Moon.* New York: Philomel.

SEQUENCE

Burleigh, Robert. 2003. *Home Run: The Story of Babe Ruth.* Boston: HMH Books.

Carle, Eric. 1994. *The Very Hungry Caterpillar.* New York: Philomel.

———. 2002. *A House for Hermit Crab.* New York: Simon Spotlight.

Cronin, Doreen. 2013. *Diary of a Spider.* New York: HarperCollins.

Crowe, Carole. 2008. *Turtle Girl.* Honesdale, PA: Boyds Mill Press.

Emerson, Judy. 2004. *Franklin Roosevelt.* Edina, MN: Capstone Press.

Floca, Brian. 2013. *Locomotive.* New York: Atheneum.

Forward, Toby. 2004. *What Did You Do Today?* New York: Clarion.

Golenbock, Peter. 2012. *ABCs of Baseball.* New York: Dial.

Hoberman, Mary Ann. 2003. *I Know an Old Lady Who Swallowed a Fly.* New York: Little, Brown Books.

Holub, Joan. 2012. *Pumpkin Countdown.* Parkridge, IL: Albert Whitman.

Jenkins, Steve. 2011. *Just a Second.* Boston: HMH Books.

Levine, Ellen. 2007. *Henry's Freedom Box.* New York: Scholastic.

Martin, Jr., Bill. 1996. *Brown Bear, Brown Bear, What Do You See?* New York: Henry Holt.

McCaughrean, Geraldine. 2002. *My Grandmother's Clock.* New York: Clarion.

Otshi, Kathryn. 2008. *One.* Novato, CA: KO Kids.

Pham, LeUyen. 2014. *A Piece of Cake.* New York: Balzer-Bray.

Rappaport, Doreen. 2014. *Lady Liberty: A Biography.* Somerville, MA: Candlewick Press.

Sturges, Philemon. 2002. *The Little Red Hen (Makes a Pizza).* New York: Puffin.

Willems, Mo. 2010. *City Dog, Country Frog.* New York: Disney-Hyperion.

Wood, Audrey. 2000. *The Napping House.* Boston: HMH Books.

Woodson, Jacqueline. 2013. *This Is the Rope*. New York: Nancy Paulsen Books.

Viorst, Judith. 1987. *Alexander and the Terrible, Horrible, No Good, Very Bad Day*. New York: Atheneum.

Young, Ed. 2002. *Seven Blind Mice*. New York: Philomel.

PROBLEM AND SOLUTION

Cronin, Doreen. 2011. *Click, Clack, Moo: Cows That Type*. New York: Simon and Schuster.

Henkes, Kevin. 2008. *Chrysanthemum*. New York: Greenwillow.

Hest, Amy. 2007. *Mr. George Baker*. Somerville, MA: Candlewick Press.

Laminack, Lester. 2002. *Trevor's Wiggly-Wobbly Tooth*. Atlanta: Peachtree.

Mochizuki, Ken. 1993. *Baseball Saved Us*. New York: Lee & Low Books.

Munson, Derek. 2000. *Enemy Pie*. San Francisco: Chronicle Books.

COMPARE AND CONTRAST

Cannon, Janell. 1993. *Stellaluna*. New York: Scholastic.

Jenkins, Steve. 2008. *What Do You Do with a Tail Like This?* Boston: Houghton Mifflin.

Pallotta, Jerry. 2010. *Who Would Win? Killer Whale vs. Great White Shark*. New York: Scholastic.

———. 2011. *Who Would Win? Hammerhead vs. Bull Shark*. New York: Scholastic.

Rodman, MaryAnn. 2008. *First Grade Stinks!* Atlanta: Peachtree.

St. George, Judith. 2005. *Take the Lead, George Washington*. New York: Philomel.

———. 2008. *Stand Tall, Abe Lincoln*. New York: Philomel.

Warren, Heather. 2011. *Brown Bear or Black Bear?* King of Prussia, PA: ARC Press.

Woodson, Jacqueline. 2001. *The Other Side*. New York: G.P. Putnam's Sons.

CAUSE AND EFFECT

Bunting, Eve. 1992. *The Wall*. New York: Clarion.

Garland, Sherry. 1997. *The Lotus Seed*. Boston: Harcourt Brace.

Henkes, Kevin. 2008. *Chrysanthemum*. New York: Greenwillow.

Numeroff, Laura Joffe. 2010. *If You Give a Mouse a Cookie*. New York: HarperCollins.

Polacco, Patricia. 1998. *My Rotten Redheaded Older Brother*. New York: Aladdin.

Weaving Meaning

INFERRING

Brinckloe, Julie. 1986. *Fireflies!* New York: Simon and Schuster.

Bunting, Eve. 2005. *Gleam and Glow*. Boston: Harcourt.

Havill, Juanita. 1987. *Jamaica's Find*. Boston: Houghton Mifflin.

Rappaport, Doreen. 2012. *Helen's Big World! The Life of Helen Keller*. New York: Hyperion.

Wyeth, Sharon Dennis. 2002. *Something Beautiful*. New York: Bantam Doubleday.

SUMMARIZING

Arnosky, Jim. 2008. *All About Frogs*. New York: Scholastic.

Brinckloe, Julie. 1986. *Fireflies!* New York: Simon and Schuster.

Brimner, Larry Dane. 2010. *Birmingham Sunday*. Columbus, OH: Highlights Press.

Jenkins, Martin. 2002. *The Emperor's Egg*. Somerville, MA: Candlewick Press.

Lyon, George Ella. 1999. *Where I'm From*. Spring, TX: Absey & Company.

———. 2003. *Mother to Tigers*. New York: Simon and Schuster.

SYNTHESIZING

Allen, Judy. 2004. *Are You a Bee?* New York: Kingfisher.

Bunting, Eve. 1999. *Smoky Night*. Boston: Harcourt Brace.

Gibbons, Gail. 2000. *The Honey Makers*. New York: HarperCollins.

Prince, April Jones. 2005. *Twenty-One Elephants and Still Standing*. Boston: Houghton Mifflin.

Rockwell, Anne. 2005. *Honey in a Hive*. New York: HarperCollins.

Wiles, Deborah. 2005. *Freedom Summer*. New York: Aladdin.

Young, Ed. 2002. *Seven Blind Mice*. New York: Philomel.

VISUALIZING

Henkes, Kevin. 2009. *Birds*. New York: Greenwillow.

Jenkins, Martin. 2002. *The Emperor's Egg*. Somerville, MA: Candlewick Press.

Johnston, Tony. 2014. *Winter Is Coming*. New York: Simon and Schuster.

Lionni, Leo. 1973. *Frederick*. Decorah, IA: Dragonfly.

MacLachlan, Patricia. 2014. *The Iridescence of Birds: A Book About Henri Matisse*. New York: Roaring Brook Press.

Nicholls, Judith. 2002. *Billywise*. New York: Bloomsbury Publishing.

Viorst, Judith. 1999. "Stanley the Fierce" in *The 20th Century Children's Poetry Treasury*, ed. Jack Prelutsky. New York: Alfred A. Knopf.

NOTICING IMPORTANT DETAILS

Cherry, Lynne. 2000. *The Great Kapok Tree*. Boston: Voyager/Harcourt.

Floca, Brian. 2013. *Locomotive*. New York: Atheneum.

Hatkoff, Craig. 2014. *Hope for Winter: The True Story of a Remarkable Friendship*. New York: Scholastic.

Havill, Juanita. 1987. *Jamaica's Find*. Boston: Houghton Mifflin.

McCully, Emily Arnold. 1996. *The Bobbin Girl*. New York: Dial.

Weatherford, Carole Boston. 2007. *Birmingham, 1963*. Honesdale, PA: Wordsong.

MAKING CONNECTIONS

Bildner, Phil. 2014. *The Soccer Fence: A True Story of Friendship, Hope, and Apartheid in South Africa*. New York: Putnam.

Boelts, Maribeth. 2009. *Those Shoes*. Somerville, MA: Candlewick Press.

Browne, Anthony. 2014. *What If . . . ?* Somerville, MA: Candlewick Press.

Fleischman, Paul. 2013. *The Matchbox Diary*. Somerville, MA: Candlewick Press.

McPhail, David. 2005. *The Teddy Bear*. New York: Square Fish.

Nolen, Jerdine. 2001. *In My Momma's Kitchen*. New York: Amistad.

Viorst, Judith. 1987. *Alexander and the Terrible, Horrible, No Good, Very Bad Day*. New York: Macmillan.

Story Elements

CHARACTER

Hest, Amy. 2003. *When Jessie Came Across the Sea*. Somerville, MA: Candlewick Press.

Keats, Ezra Jack. 1976. *The Snowy Day*. New York: Puffin.

———. 1998. *Whistle for Willie*. Pine Plains, NY: Live Oak Media.

———. 1998. *Peter's Chair*. New York: Puffin.

Paterson, Katherine. 2004. *The Great Gilly Hopkins*. New York: HarperCollins.

Rylant, Cynthia. 1996. *An Angel for Solomon Singer*. New York: Orchard/Scholastic.

Slade, Suzanne. 2014. *With Books and Bricks: How Booker T. Washington Built a School*. Park Ridge, IL: Albert Whitman.

White, E. B. 2012. *Charlotte's Web*. New York: HarperCollins.

SETTING

Crews, Donald. 1998. *BigMama's*. New York: Scholastic.

Frazee, Marla. 2006. *Roller Coaster*. Boston: Harcourt, Inc.

Johnston, Tony. 2014. *Sequoia*. New York: Roaring Brook.

Keats, Ezra Jack. 1999. *Apt. 3*. New York: Puffin.

MacLachlan, Patricia. 1994. *All the Places to Love*. New York: HarperCollins.

PLOT

Fox, Mem. 2000. *Feathers and Fools*. Boston: Harcourt Brace.

Keats, Ezra Jack. 1998. *Peter's Chair*. New York: Puffin.

Munson, Derek. 2000. *Enemy Pie.* San Francisco: Chronicle.

Say, Allen. 2008. *Grandfather's Journey.* New York: Scholastic.

Zee, Ruth Vander. 2013. *Erika's Story.* Mankato, MN: Creative Editions.

PERSPECTIVE AND POINT OF VIEW

Asim, Jaban. 2012. *Fifty Cents and a Dream: Young Booker T. Washington.* New York: Little, Brown and Co.

Henkes, Kevin. 1995. *Julius: The Baby of the World.* New York: Greenwillow.

Hest, Amy. 2013. *When Charley Met Grampa.* Somerville, MA: Candlewick Press.

Lehrhaupt, Adam. 2013. *Do Not Open This Book!* New York: Simon and Schuster.

Lyon, George Ella. 1998. *A Sign.* New York: Orchard.

Kearnly, Meg. 2013. *Trouper.* New York: Scholastic.

Nichols, Lori. 2014. *Maple and Willow Together.* New York: Penguin.

Reagan, Jean. 2014. *How to Babysit a Grandma!* New York: Alfred A. Knopf.

Rubin, Adam. 2013. *Secret Pizza Party.* New York: Dial.

Snead, Philip C. 2010. *A Sick Day for Amos McGee.* New York: Roaring Brook Press.